On the Origin o
& Evolution

ISBN 978-1-935786-28-3

Published in the United States of America

St. Clair Publications
P. O. Box 726
Mc Minnville, TN 37111-0726
http://stclairpublications.com

On the Origin of the Clichés

& Evolution of Idioms

Illustrated

Stanley J. St. Clair

On the Origin of the Clichés & Evolution of Idioms

INTRODUCTION

This book is a serious adventure in humorous phrase origins and **etymology,** both for the education and entertainment of the reader. It was based on miscellaneous data from a large variety of sources, often utilizing two or more of them in a single entry. Charles Darwin wrote a book with a similar title, and shook a lot of folks up. I put my unique personality into this work, and tried to make it intriguing enough to read all the way through. To interest persons of all ages, I chose phrases which most of us have heard, especially in America. All effort was exerted to be as accurate as possible in the determination of origins and meanings. It was composed in the hope that it could bring smiles to its readers, along with a deeper appreciation and sense of understanding of our ever-evolving English jargon. It contains almost four hundred **clichés, idioms, axioms, proverbs, similes, old sayings and curious words and catch-phrases** which are, and have been, in the popular culture of English-speaking peoples in various sections of America and the United Kingdom. I hope all who read it enjoy pouring through these pages. A bibliography follows in order as indicated which includes 43 dictionaries and reference works, 94 other books, 26 biblical texts, 65 citations from newspapers, magazines and

journals, 28 film, television and radio references, 14 plays, 17 songs, 20 narrative poems,
and 14 miscellaneous items utilized including
currency, court records, letters, etc. as well as
scores of web sites accessed as a starting point
to find the true origins and meanings.

Definitions

from Dictionary.com

Etymology – The derivation of a word.

Cliché - a trite, stereotyped expression; a sentence or a phrase usually expressing a popular or common thought or idea that has lost originality, ingenuity and impact by long overuse, as *sadder but wiser*, or *strong as an ox*.

Idiom - an expression whose meaning is not predictable from the usual meanings of its constituent elements, as *kick the bucket* or *hang one's head*, or from the general grammatical rules of a language, as *the table round* for *the round table*, and that is not a constituent of a larger expression of like characteristics.

Axiom – a self-evident truth that requires no proof.

Proverb - a short popular saying, usually of unknown and ancient origin, that expresses effectively some commonplace truth or useful thought; adage.

Simile – A figure of speech in which two unlike things are explicitly compared, as in "she is like a rose."

Not in dictionary.com – explanations

Old saying – a phrase of obscure origin which has become a part of popular jargon.

Curious words and catch-phrases – expressions which are often used, whether as a single word or a phrase, which seem strange as to their exact origin or meaning and need clarification.

A

"Absence makes the heart grow fonder"

Ah, yes, let's begin our adventure by dabbling in the controversial sentimentality of ancient wisdom in cementing love.

The heart of this proverb has been present in culture since the days of the Roman Empire near the turn of the last age. The poet Sextus Propertius gave the world the earliest form of this saying in his work, *Elegies*. Properly translated to modern English, it read:

> "Always toward absent lovers love's tide stronger flows."

The Pocket Magazine of Classics and Polite Literature, in 1832, printed a contemporary version attributed to a Miss Strickland.

> "'Tis absence, however, that makes the heart grow fonder."

The proverb can be used to mean that the lack of anything can make the desire for it grow stronger. Hmm. This *may* be true.

"All dressed up with no place to go"

This common saying has a variety of meanings, all somewhat connected. It can infer that you are working hard, but have no plan or goal for yourself. It can also mean that you are expecting something to happen that just isn't going to materialize, like waiting for your 'ship to come in' when you haven't sent one out. Have you ever wished you could win the lottery when you didn't even buy a ticket? Or, it could, and does mean in certain cases, something a bit more literal: you look good, but don't have anywhere to show off your new clothes, etc.

At any rate, you need to change your method and make a new plan. The phrase was coined in America, and has been around for many years. It was popular in the 1960s and '70s and is still used today.

"All in the same boat"

When I heard this in the 1944 World War II movie, *Lifeboat*, starring Tallulah Bankhead, I wondered if that may have been its origin. How wrong I was. This phrase has been around since the age of Ancient Greece, and has been used figuratively for centuries.

On the Origin of the Clichés & Evolution of Idioms

In 1862, Artemus Ward used this in *The Draft in Baldwinsville*. 'We are all in the same boat.'

This phrase means that when we realize that someone else is in the same circumstances as we, the best alternative is cooperation on reaching a solution to the common challenges.

"All that glitters is not gold"

Wow, this conjures up some old memories for me. Not of gold, mind you, but of studying *The Merchant of Venice* in high school. The original was actually 'glisters' rather than glitters, but the rest was in tact as penned by Shakespeare in 1586. Hey, it's only one letter different. I have enclosed the entire verse.

> MOROCCO:
> O hell! what have we here?
> A carrion Death, within whose empty eye
> There is a written scroll! I'll read the writing.
> All that glitters is not gold;
> Often have you heard that told:
> Many a man his life hath sold
> But my outside to behold:
> Gilded tombs do worms enfold.
> Had you been as wise as bold,
> Young in limbs, in judgment old,

Your answer had not been inscroll'd:
Fare you well; your suit is cold.

This has come to symbolize the constant struggle of humanity to seek for prosperity, and in so doing, often 'grab at straws' (see) which appear to be ways to 'get rich quick.' Just because something looks good doesn't mean that it is — usually it is quite the opposite.

William Shakespeare

1564-1616

Phrases in this book are linked to 12 plays attributed to him.

"All things come to he who waits"

This proverb is a good one to follow 'all that glitters in not gold.' It, also is very old, and may be a takeoff on a biblical verse from *Isaiah 40:31.*

> "But they that wait upon the Lord shall renew their strength..."

Though she did not likely originate the saying, it was used by Violet Fane (1843-1905) in her poem *Tout vient a qui sait attendre.*

> "'Ah, all things come to those who wait,'
> (I say these words to make me glad),
> But something answers soft and sad,
> 'They come, but often come too late.'"

"apple a day keeps the doctor away, An"

Reference to this was first found in a Welsh folk proverb."Eat an apple on going to bed, and you'll keep the doctor from eating his bread." The phrase was first coined as we know it in the US in 1913.

"Apple of my eye"

This idiom comes from the *Bible*. In *Psalm 17:8* the psalmist asks God 'keep me as the apple of your eye.' It means the center of thoughts; one to be loved and appreciated.

"As cool as a cucumber"

One of hundreds of English similes, this one dates back to the eighteenth century. It was first recorded in John Gay's *New Song on New Similes* in 1732:

> "I...cool as a cucumber could see The rest of womanhood."

Here, cool means calm and collected rather than cool to the touch. If someone is 'cool as a cucumber' it means that they can face the most reprehensible situation without worrying if their deodorant will hold out. Pretty cool, huh?

"As dumb as a box of rocks"

Hey, this is another one of those Southern US colloquiums that every good ol' boy in the Deep South grew up with for the last hundred years or more. If someone was 'half a brick short of a load' he was 'dumber than a box of rocks.' Now what could have less of a brain than rocks?

"As easy as pie"

This phrase obviously isn't talking about baking a pie. Too many have failed miserably unless they were well-versed in the art of pie baking. This simile was coined in nineteenth century America, when it referred to the ease of eating a tasty pastry. The task was related to pleasant times when family was gathered for festive occasions. There are a number of examples, not every one in the self-same phraseology. In fact, the first known printed reference is to a variant of this, 'nice as pie,' in 1855, in an article titled *Which, Right or Left?*

> "For nearly a week afterwards, the domestics observed significantly to each other, that Miss Isabella was as nice as pie."

Mark Twain used pie in this sense several times in *The Adventures of Huckleberry Finn*, published in 1884. Here is one of those examples:

"You're always as polite as pie to them."

Mark Twain, 1907

Photo, A.F. Bradley

Also around the same time, pie became used to describe an easy task to accomplish. A reference is found in the American magazine, *Sporting Life,* in the May 1886 issue.

"As for stealing around second and third (bases), it's like eating pie."

The earliest known printing of the actual simile, 'as easy as pie' appeared in the Rhode Island newspaper, *The Newport Mercury* in June 1887, in a comical story about two New Yorkers who were down on their luck.

> "You see veuever I goes I take mit me a silverspoon or knife or some things an' I gets two or three dollars for them. It's as easy as pie. Vy don't you try it?"

Other phrases related to ease pleasantry are 'piece of cake' (see) and 'take the cake.'

"As good as gold"

Since there are far too many of these common similes to record them all in this little volume, I will select a few, 'as good as gold' being next.

In this phrase, good doesn't mean what it normally does. It refers to someone or something that is well-behaved, such as a child who has remembered his or her manners with someone the child is unaccustomed to being with.

With banknotes, which Americans know as bills, they weren't considered to be money.

They were promissory notes, like IOUs. Gold or silver, as referred to in the *Bible*, were the real money. This had the intrinsic value. In the UK, banknotes still include printed messages to this end. I'm looking at a One Pound note right now. It says, *"For the Gov.' and Comp. of the Bank of England"* which is undersigned by the Chief Cashier of the Bank of England.

'As good as gold' meant that something was genuine and to be accepted just like the real currency.

The first recorded use of this as a simile was in 1845, in Thomas Hood's poem, *The Lost Heir.*

"Sitting as good as gold in the glitter."

The present-day meaning has evolved through the years.

"As happy as a lark"

It seems there is no end to the similes which have been in circulation in the English language for hundreds of years. This is another of those. It was in use as early as the late eighteenth and early nineteenth centuries. Though other such terms such as 'happy as a clam' (mid nineteenth century) and my personal favorite, 'happy as a dead pig in the sunshine' (from the Deep South, my 'neck of the woods') have entered the speech of various segments of our American population, happy as a lark seems to have been of the longest endurance and widest usage.

As happy as a lark is derived from the cheerful song of this beautiful and common songbird. I suppose you just can't get happier than that.

"As old as Methuselah"

Yep, another phrase of biblical origin, which no doubt has been heard and even used by lots of folks who never heard of the old man except in this saying. Methuselah was recorded in *Genesis 5:21-27* as the son of Enoch, and was said to have lived to the ripe old age of 969 — the oldest man in the *Bible*.

'As old as Methuselah' has come to mean ya just can't get any older, like 'old as dirt,' and is used as a comical term about someone who is considerably more aged than the speaker. Remember everything is relative. I once asked a fifteen-year old girl how old her mother was, to which she replied, "Oh, she's old, you know, thirty-something."

"As snug as a bug in a rug"

If someone didn't know better, they may think that this rhyming metaphor came into being in the 1950s. Not so. It first appeared in print in 1769. But let's look at the meaning of this curious saying as it was in the eighteenth century. 'Snug' was then used to mean, 'neat, trim and well prepared,' specifically as it referred to ships of the day. It had been so used since at least the latter sixteenth century.

Before bugs were insects, they were ghosts or spirits. In 1535, the *Cloverdale Bible* uses it in this fashion in *Psalms 91:5*:

> "So yt thou shalt not nede to be afrayed for eny bugges by night, ner for arowe that flyeth by daye."

By 1642, however, bug also meant 'beetle' or something like it, as seen in Daniel Rogers' *Naaman the Syrian*.

> "Gods rare workmanship in the Ant, the poorest bugge that creeps."

As I mentioned in the beginning of this entry, the first known printed reference to 'as snug as a bug in a rug' was in 1769. It is in David Garrick's writings about Shakespeare called *Garrick's vagary, or, England run mad*; with particulars of the Strafford Jubilee.

> "If she [a rich widow] has the mopus's [coins or money], I'll have her, as snug as a bug in a rug."

The word 'rug' here, is a Tudor word with the same source as the word 'rag.' But then, rugs were not on the floor, but were thick woolen bed covers, what might today be blankets. So a 'bug in a rug' would have been happy and snug, indeed.

"As the crow flies"

This universal comparison was coined in the UK and has been long used in Scotland to denote the shortest route, likely because of the presence of many crows there. The choice of a crow, other than for this reason, seems inappropriate, since their flight patterns are not notable for their straightness, and they frequently fly in long arcs in search of food.

The first known printed citation is from the *London Review of English and Foreign Literature* by W. Kenrick, 1767.

> "The Spaniard, if on foot, always travels as the crow flies, which the openness and dryness of the country permits; neither rivers nor the steepest mountains stop his course, he swims over the one and scales the other."

"As ugly as homemade sin"

This one is definitely an old Appalachian mountain slang saying which goes back generations to 'no tellin' who.' I heard it when I grew up in the Blue Ridge Mountains in the fifties and sixties, and my parents heard it and so did theirs, 'I reckon.' Some folks think it refers to incest which used to be prevalent 'round those parts, but I don't think so. I never took it that way. It was just a way of sayin' whatcha thought. If somebody was ugly, they couldn't think of a worse thing to compare it to. Sin was doin' anything your mama and daddy and the Good Book said was wrong. And if'n ya couldn't find it there, then ya might make up som'thin' just 'cause it seemed like it wasn't quite up to Hoyle. Get it? Homemade sin.

"At the end of the day"

I have included this modern idiom because in the future, 'at the end of the day,' people will be looking back on the origin of this in the same way we do others in this book.

Meaning the same as the 'tried and true' (see) or saying 'after all is said and done,' it did not come into popular usage until the early twenty-first century, although it could have been around in limited speech a bit earlier.

"Aw Pshaw!"

The dictionaries, including *Merriam Webster*, list pshaw as an expression of irritation, contempt, disgust or disapproval. Though antiquated, and replaced by other terms of utter disgust, I like to put it with aw, because that is how I heard my grandfather say it when I was a kid. He was of a long line of mountain folk from the hills of North and South Carolina. At least some of his ancestors were from Scotland. *Merriam Webster* says it has been around since 1656. Since that's a specific year, I'm quite certain that was in reference to a particular book... Could it possibly be Thomas Blount's *Glossographia*? Since Blount was, among other professions, a lexicographer, and this tome was a dictionary of over 11,000 words published that year, this seems likely, though I have not seen the text. In 1777, here is a quote using the saying from Richard B. Sheridan, in *School for Scandal*:

"Pshaw! He is too moral by half!"

"axe to grind, An"

One source, *The Phrase Finder*, says that this comes from a story by our old friend, Ben Franklin, who wrote his autobiography some-where between 1771 and 1780, when he died. In it, this source states, was a tale about a man who asked a smith to sharpen his axe especially well. According to the tale, the stranger ended up doing most of the grinding himself.

According to myth, however, when Ben Franklin was just a young man, he was approached by a stranger who stopped to admire the family grindstone. The stranger expressed great interest in the simple device and asked Ben to show him how it worked by sharpening one of his axes for him. Once the axe was nice and sharp, the stranger walked away laughing merrily at his ingenious ploy. This explanation made more sense to me.

A reference which uses the phrase as we know it came a few years later (1811) in *Who'll turn Grindstones* by Charles Miner.

"When I see a merchant over-polite to his customers ... thinks I, that man has an axe to grind."

The saying now means that someone has 'a method behind their madness' (see) or a hidden reason for their actions. Often they are seeking revenge against someone.

B

"Back in the day"

This is the latest rendition of a tradition which started long ago. This phrase, per se, evolved in the latter part of the twentieth century by young to middle-aged urban Americans referring to the era in which they were growing up, likely 'in the hood' (see). To pin it down is a near impossibility.

Immediately before this, the phrase 'back in my day' was popular, and prior to *that*, 'in the old days' or in the 'good old days.' Since all of these are related phrases, I will not give a separate section to the others. In time relation, it is like thinking that the 'grass is greener on the other side of the fence.' People naturally relate to the days of their youth as their prime time—as an era when life was better and they could 'write their own ticket.' I didn't believe my mother when I was a teenager and she told me, "Son, these are the best years of your life." Oh, mama mia!

"Back to the drawing board"

On 1 March 1941 the cartoon below, drawn by famed American cartoonist Peter Arno (Curtis Arnoux Peters, Jr.) was published by *New Yorker Magazine.* It depicts a World War II plane crashing in plain view of spectators. Little did they know that the caption, 'Well, it's back to the old drawing board,' would create a cliché which would be used by their generation, and likely all generations to come.

"Well, back to the old drawing board."

"Baker's dozen"

This old saying is said to come from the days when bakers were severely punished for baking underweight loaves. Some added an extra loaf to a batch of a dozen to be above suspicion. A baker's dozen thus means thirteen.

"ball's in your court, The"

Meaning, 'It's your turn to make a move' (I've done all I can do), this slogan is a metaphor for the tennis ball, etc. being on your side of the net. This sports idiom crept into general usage in the second half of the twentieth century. The first printing of it seems elusive.

"Bang for the buck"

This saying, which means 'value for one's money,' was originally a political phrase. With 'bang' referring to 'firepower' or 'weaponry,' it literally meant 'bombs for one's money.' The alliteration of 'bang' and 'buck' helps to make the phrase memorable.

The earliest confirmed reference to 'bang for the buck' is found in 1968 in the first edition of William Safire's *New Language of Politics*. Safire claims that the phrase was coined in 1954 by Charles E. Wilson, the Secretary of Defense, in reference to the "massive retaliation" policy of then Secretary of State, John Foster Dulles.

While 'bang' has been used in a sexual sense from as far back as the seventeenth century, it is unrelated to this phrase. However, since people are always eager to give things sexual connotations whether or not they are intended, some prudence would be a wise idea.

Rephrased from information found in *The Mavens' Word of the Day* (December 19, 1997).

The phrase has certainly been used in all cases relating to getting more out of an investment of money or time.

"Baptism by fire"

When I heard this yesterday on a popular TV show, it made me think of its origin from the biblical book of *Matthew*, in *chapter 3, verse 11*. The words are attributed to John the Baptist.

"I indeed baptize you with water unto repentance, but he that cometh after me is mightier than I, whose shoes I am not worthy to bear: he shall baptize you with the Holy Ghost and with fire."

There are differing beliefs as to the baptism by fire mentioned here (some say power from God, some say persecution and martyrdom).

As an idiom in our modern world, a 'baptism by fire' means our worst nightmare has come true. It applies to the tests that life may bring our way to make us better people. Though this type of adversity is something to which we do not look forward, if we hold up and come through it, it can change our entire lives for the better.

"Bated breath"

Well, it seems like a lot of folks have trouble understanding this one, as some want to spell it 'baited,' even to J.K. Rowling in the Harry Potter novel, *The Prisoner of Azkaban*. However, it really should be 'bated,' as this is merely a shortened form of abated, meaning brought down, lowered or depressed. Bated breath is breathing that is subdued because of an emotional difficulty. Most often someone is likely to say, "I'll be waiting with bated breath," meaning that they will be anxiously anticipating an answer or response.

Here is another example of Shakespeare's ability to pass down a cliché. The first reference is in *The Merchant of Venice*:

"What should I say to you? Should I not say
'Hath a dog money? is it possible
A cur can lend three thousand ducats?' Or
Shall I bend low and in a bondman's key,
With bated breath and whispering
humbleness, Say this;
'Fair sir, you spit on me on Wednesday last;
You spurn'd me such a day; another time
You call'd me dog; and for these courtesies
I'll lend you thus much moneys'?"

It makes me want to wait with bated breath for the next performance of one of Shakespeare's magnificent plays.

"Bats in the belfry"

Can't you just hear this phrase in an old British movie, or imagine reading it in a Gothic novel from the nineteenth century? Well, guess again. The phrase was originated in the US in the early twentieth century. Bats are busy little blind winged mammals which fly about in dark places. Belfries, of course, are in towers like church steeples, and were places in which bats dwelt. The earliest record of this phrase is from American writers from just after the beginning of the twentieth century. For example, this is from an article in *The Newark Daily Advocate*, in Ohio, not New Jersey, in October 1900:

"To his hundreds of friends and acquaint-tances in Newark, these purile [sic] and senseless attacks on Hon. John W. Cassingham are akin to the vaporings of the fellow with a large flock of bats in his belfry."

The usage here has continued to this day. Someone who is confused and a bit dazzled may be said to have 'bats in the belfry,' or 'gone bats.'

"Beat around the bush"

When hunting birds there was a common practice in olden days of taking a stick and beating around (or about) bushes to drive birds out into the open. Afterward, someone would attempt to catch the birds. 'I won't beat about the bush' came to mean 'I will get straight to the point without any delay.'

It first appeared in print in the medieval poem, *Generydes, A Romance in Seven Fine Stanzas,* in about 1440.

> "Butt as it hath be sayde full long agoo,
> Some bete the bussh and some the byrdes take."

The poet is unknown and the only copy is a single handwritten manuscript in the library of Trinity College in Cambridge in the UK.

Even in this poem, it is clear that beating the bush was a poor substitute for actually getting on with the hunt and taking the birds.

Then, in 1572, George Gascoigne adds 'about' to the phrase in *Works.*

> "He bet about the bush, whyles other caught the birds."

"Beauty is only skin deep"

It never ceases to amaze me how many of these proverbs date from the seventeenth century and earlier. This one is attributed to Thomas Overbury. The text is in *Overbury's Wife*, 1613, published, 1614:

> "All the carnall beautie of my wife, Is but skinne-deep."

Other references attributed to Overbury carry the same meaning.

A poem by John Daves, *A Select Second Husband,* in 1616, states:

> "Beauty's but skin-deepe."

Many references have occurred since. The saying means that though outward beauty is alluring, it does not determine the true worth or character of the person. A related phrase is 'Beauty is as beauty does.'

"Bee line"

In past centuries most people believed that bees always flew in a straight line to their hives. Therefore, making a 'bee line' for something came to mean going straight for it.

"Before you could say Jack Robinson'

Of course we know the meaning of this expression to be 'suddenly, with lightening speed.' I don't know how long it takes me to say Jack Robinson, but I can hardly imagine that it is longer than a couple of seconds.

It is likely that this 'Jack Robinson' was just as mythical as Jack Frost or Jack be nimble, or the Jacks of all trades. However, some have suggested that John Robinson, the Constable of the Tower of London in the late seventeenth century at a time when heads were quickly chopped off, was the inspiration for this famous or *infamous* Jack.

At any rate, in 1778, Fanny Burney used a form of it in her romantic novel, *Evelina, or the history of a young lady's entrance into the world.*

> "'For the matter of that there,' said the Captain, 'you must make him a soldier, before you can tell which is lightest, head or heels. Howsomever, I'd lay ten pounds to a shilling, I could whisk him so

dexterously over into the pool, that he should light plump upon his foretop and turn round like a tetotum.'

"'Done!' cried Lord Merton; 'I take your odds.'

"'Will you?' returned he; 'why, then, 'fore George, I'd do it as soon as say Jack Robinson.'"

"Beggars can't be choosers"

Like the other proverb in this book with a similar meaning, 'you can't look a gift horse in the mouth' (see) this was recorded and passed down to us by John Heywood, this one in his 1562 book of Proverbs. In Heywood's day, there was very little pity and provision for the poor, and if one were fortunate enough to be the recipient of a gift, he should appreciate it, even if it did not completely meet the need at hand. Here is the quote from Heywood.

"Beggers should be no choosers, but yet they will:

Who can bryng a begger from choyse to begge still?"

The actual meaning at the time was 'beggars ought not to be choosers, rather than 'can't be.'

"Bent out of shape"

This expression for being extremely upset about something is very new by the standards of most in this book. It never came into practical usage until the second half of the nineteenth century.

Bob Dylan used the phrase in his long satiric lyric *It's Alright Ma (I'm Only Bleeding)*, "Bent out of shape from society's pliers..." This is probably the genesis of its acceptance into pop culture jargon.

"Better a friend who is close than a brother far away"

This is likely the way you have heard this proverb, but it is actually a paraphrase of a biblical proverb from King Solomon in *Proverbs 27:10*. Actually, this is very close to the *New American Standard Version* of last part of this verse:

"Do not forsake your own friend or your father's friend, And do not go to your brother's house in the day of your calamity; **Better is a neighbor who is near than a brother far away.**"

The saying is pretty much an axiom. Sometimes having a friend or neighbor close in time of need is better than having to go a great distance for a family member who may not even be as willing to help as your friend.

"Better late than never"

Well, I should have composed and published this book years ago, but 'better late than never.' This is just the type of sarcasm expressed when this all-too-frequent proverb is blurted out. The first citation to it seems to have been by Geoffrey Chaucer in *Canterbury Tales*, which lies on my bookshelf collecting dust. It's from the story titled *Yeoman's Prologue*, about 1386. Of course it is Old English.

"For bot than never is late'"

"Between a rock and a hard place"

The basis of this expression has been said to arise from the Greek Classics. Odysseus, it is written, had to pass between the monster, Scylla, and the deadly whirlpool Charydbis.

The phrase itself, however, is of American origin and was first recorded in *Dialect Notes V* in 1921.

> "To be between a rock and a hard place…to be bankrupt. Common in Arizona in recent panics; sporadic in California."

The 'recent panics' mentioned here no doubt refer to the events surrounding the Bisbee, Arizona mine worker deportations of 1917. Early in the twentieth century a dispute developed between the copper mining companies and the mine workers. In 1917, the workers, some of which had organized labor unions, presented a list of demands, including more pay and better working conditions, to their bosses. Their demands were refused and many workers were deported to New Mexico. It is believed that the choice of these workers between poor working conditions at the rockface, and unemployment inspired the original saying, 'between a rock and a hard place.'

"Beyond the pale"

If someone is beyond the pale, they are incorrigible — beyond the acceptable standards of decency.

This may be better understood in Europe and the UK than the US. Originally a pale was an area under the authority of a certain ruler or government official.

In the fourteenth and fifteenth centuries the King of England ruled Dublin and the surrounding area known as the *Pale of Dublin*. The *Pale of Calais* was formed in France as early as 1360. Catherine the Great created a *Pale of Settlement* in Russia in 1791.

A pale has long been associated with a fence in which one is protected; a safe, enclosed area. Anyone 'beyond the pale' was seen as savage and dangerous.

"Beyond the shadow of a doubt"

After doing some digging I found out that a forerunner of this has been around since circa 1300. According to Christine Ammer in *The American Heritage Dictionary of Idioms*, the simple form, 'beyond a doubt' dates to that year. Other early references appear as 'shadow of a doubt,' sans the word beyond.

In 1850, Nathaniel Hawthorne included 'the shadow of a doubt' in *The Scarlet Letter.*

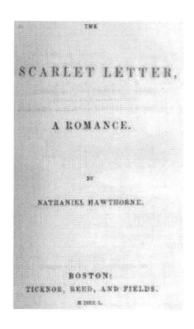

Then, the popular source for most researchers on the full phrase, 'beyond the shadow of a doubt' is Robert Frost in his brilliant poem, *The Trial by Existence* in 1915.

Harper Lee's highly acclaimed *To Kill a Mockingbird* included Atticus Finch's well-known court statement:

"The law says 'reasonable doubt,' but I think a defendant's entitled to the shadow of a doubt. There's always the possibility, no matter how improbable, that he's innocent."

This suggests that a 'shadow of a doubt' exceeds the requirement of law in court cases determining guilt.

British historian and businessman, Niven Sinclair, released parts of a yet-unpublished extensive document in 1996 as a two-part series in the Clan Sinclair Canada Association official publication, *Roslin O Roslin,* the total being titled *Beyond Any Shadow of Doubt.* It documents what he feels are conclusive proofs of a 1398 voyage by his ancestor, Jarl 'Prince' Henry St. Clair to the New World from Orkney, the northernmost islands of Scotland.

"Biblical proportions"

This is one most of us never heard when we were growing up, even though some of us were told about the actual biblical examples used to inspire the term.

Talk of events being 'of biblical proportions' meaning 'exceptionally large scale disasters,' has been documented back as far as the 1980s. One such example is from the movie, *Ghostbusters* (1989), when Dr. Peter Venkman, played by Bill Murray, said to the mayor, "Or can you accept the fact that this city is headed for a disaster of biblical proportions?"

Other examples are found in such publications as *Time Magazine*. Since then, the idiom has become utilized in pop culture to describe Armageddon-type cataclysms feared to happen, and actual disasters such as tsunamis and especially devastating hurricanes and tornadoes. The news media has eaten this phrase up and uses it freely.

"Big Wig"

Centuries ago, incredibly, men and women took baths only twice a year, traditionally in May and October. Women always kept their hair covered, while men shaved their heads to avoid lice and bugs and wore wigs. Wealthy men could afford high-quality wigs made from wool. They were not able to wash the wigs, so to clean them they would carve out a loaf of bread, put the wig in the shell, and bake it for thirty minutes. The heat would make the wig big and fluffy; hence the term 'big wig.' Today people often use the term 'Big Wig' to describe a person who appears to be powerful and wealthy.

"bird in the hand is worth two in the bush, A"

This common proverb, meaning a small advantage or known asset is more valuable to a chance at a larger profit goes back to medieval days when falcons were commonly used as birds of prey. It meant that the falcon was very valuable to its owner and certainly worth more than two birds not yet obtained (in the bush).

The first reference in print to the term as it is currently used was in John Ray's *A Hand-book of Proverbs*, published in 1670. How far back it was actually in use is debated. A similar proverb is found in Solomon's biblical book of *Ecclesiastes* chapter 9, verse 4. 'A living dog is better than a dead lion.' This was quoted by Henry David Thoreau in *Conclusion*, from *Walden*.

An even closer version is quoted in a book of proverbs by John Heywood in 1546 titled *A dialogue conteinying the number in effect of all the prouerbes in the Englishe tongue.* This version was printed as: 'Better one byrde in the hande than ten in the wood.'

'The Bird in Hand' was used as a common name for English pubs in the Middle Ages, and several still exist with the name. In 1734, a hamlet in Pennsylvania was founded with that name.

"Birds of a feather flock together"

Meaning that persons of similar interests are likely to find each other and keep company, the phrase has been around at least since the mid sixteenth century. William Turner used a form of it in his 'papist satire' (writing against the Roman Catholic religion) *The Rescuing of Romish Fox.*

"Byrdes of an kynde and coulor flok and flye always together."

"Bite the bullet"

This old saying comes from the days before anesthetics. A soldier about to undergo an operation was given a bullet to bite. It now means to grin and bear a painful situation. It can also mean missing the worst case scenario.

"Bite the dust"

This well-known phrase doesn't originate with American Western movies. Its earliest printed non-English reference comes from of the epic Ancient Greek poem, Homer's *Iliad* about the Trojan War with the Greeks, written circa 700 BC, translated in the nineteenth century. To 'bite the dust' was a poetic way of describing the death of a warrior. Homer or translator?

> "Grant that my sword may pierce the shirt of Hector about his heart, and that full many of his comrades may bite the dust as they fall dying round him."

The first citation of the phrase in English came from the Scottish author-translator, Tobias Smollatt, in 1750, in *Adventures of Gil Blas of Santillane*:

"We made two of them bite the dust, and the others betake themselves to flight."

"Black as the ace of spades"

The ace of spades has a special significance because in England, many years ago, playing cards were taxed. To be certain that the tax was paid by card companies, it was illegal for anyone but the government to print the ace of spades, then the card companies had to buy these from the government, thus paying the tax.

The card was, of course, black, but it was made especially ornate which made its black color stand out. Thus, the phrase came to be, as 'black as the ace of spades.'

"Blessing in disguise"

This line has been in usage in English at least since the eighteenth century, and the earliest known reference to it was by British writer and clergyman, James Hervey, in *Reflections on a Flower Garden*, 1746.

It clearly means that when a circumstance seems to be adverse, often the 'cloud has a silver lining' (see) and it will turn out to be a blessing. It reminds me of the popular Garth Brooks song, *Unanswered Prayers*. This lyric, based on a true story, tells of a man who wanted to marry his high school sweetheart, and it turned out that he didn't and he was blessed to marry another lady who became the love of his life. After a chance meeting with the previous girlfriend at a high school football game, he thanks God that he didn't marry her.

"Blind leading the blind"

This one, like many common sayings, is from the *Bible*. In *Matthew 15:14*, Jesus criticized the Pharisees, who were the religious authorities of his day, saying they were 'blind leaders of the blind.'

"Blue-bloods"

I'm not referring to the TV show starring Tom Selleck. This term means aristocratic. For centuries Arabs occupied Spain, but they were gradually forced out during the Middle Ages.

The upper class of Spain had lighter skin than most of the population, as their ancestors had not inter-married with the occupying Arabs. As a result, the blue-looking blood running through their veins was more visible. Of course we know that all blood is red, but it sometimes appears to be blue when veins are visible near the skin's surface. As a result, blue-blooded came to mean "upper class."

"Boys will be boys"

This Old English expression has been around for a very long time, but not as long as 'boys have been boys.' This expression apparently was in print as early as 1589. Around the beginning of the seventeenth century, Thomas Deloney, in *The Gentle Craft*, made the statement a bit more generalized by stating, 'Youth will be youth.' (The version I have seen is a later printing, dated 1903.)

In 1935, a British comedy film was made named *Boys Will be Boys*, and several rock groups have recorded songs by that name. There was even a short-run American TV sitcom, which began as *Second Chance* and revamped as *Boys will be Boys* in 1988.

The term implies that there are certain intrinsic characteristics which apply to all young male humans which remain constant, and we may as well accept them for who they are and let nature take its course. It has been used by parents and well-meaning friends of young boys for generation after generation; but for those enduring their antics, it gets no easier to bear. When my children (2 boys and 2 girls) were teenagers, I told them that I had learned that teen age was a disease, and I would be glad when it was cured, so I agree with Thomas Deloney.

"Break a leg"

This idiom seems related to an oxymoron, for it states the exact opposite of what is being intended. It is utilized in the theater, reportedly out of the superstition that it was bad luck to wish an actor good luck before a show. It is most often used before the opening night of a play.

This oldest of uses supposedly has origins in ancient Greece and Rome. It is said that in ancient Greece spectators in the arenas would stomp rather than clap, and they would sometimes break a leg.

In ancient Rome, gladiators would fight to the death in the Colosseum. One source says that spectators would shout, "quasso cruris," the Latin equivalent of 'break a leg.' This was said to be suggesting that the gladiators stay alive by only breaking the leg of their opponents.

Other ethnic origins are also reported, such as Elizabethan theater, Yiddish (Hatsloche un Broche) and German/Polish beginnings (połamania nóg). At any rate, it seems a universal saying which dates far back into the history of our world.

'Break a leg' also can mean, 'make a strenuous effort.' There are many references in which it is used this way as well. One is from the *Evening State Journal* in Nebraska in 1937.

"With all the break-a-leg dancing there are many who still warm to graceful soft shoe stepping."

Another such citation is from *The Hammond Times* in Indiana in 1942.

"Whatever the army or navy want, the Continental Roll [and Steel Foundry] will turn out ... Or break a leg trying."

"Break the ice"

All cities that grew from trade because they were built on rivers suffered when the cold winters froze over their gateway to the world. Small ships were developed to break the ice to 'forge a path for others to follow' so the large ships could get in and bring their precious cargoes.

The first recorded figurative use of this phrase, meaning 'to prepare the way' for anything, or to create a good relationship with a stranger, was by Thomas North in his 1579 translation of *Plutarch's Lives of the noble Grecians and Romanes.*

> "The Oratour - At last broke silence, and the ice."

"Bring home the bacon"

The roots of this common phrase may go as far back in the annals of history as early twelfth century Essex, to the story of the 'Dunmow Flitch,' when a tradition was begun in 1104 which continues to this day. It is based on a local couple who impressed the Prior of Little Dunmow with their devotion to each other in marriage to the point that he awarded them a flitch (a side) of bacon. The ritual of presenting devoted couples a flitch each year is well documented and mentioned in Geoffrey Chaucer's *The Wife of Bath's Tale and Prolouge* in 1395. They are a part of *The Canterbury Tales* which I proudly have in my library.

> "But never for us the flitch of bacon though,
> That some may win in Essex at Dunmow."

A woodcut from William Caxton's 2nd Edition of *The Canterbury Tales* **printed 1483.**

In early American county fairs, greased pig contests were held, and the winner kept the little porker, and 'took home the bacon.'

When Joe Gans and Oliver Nelson fought for the World Heavyweight Championship in 1906, the New York newspaper, *The Post Standard* reported on September 4th:

"Before the fight Gans received a telegram from his mother: 'Joe, the eyes of the world are on you. Everybody says you ought to win. Peter Jackson will tell me the news and you bring home the bacon.'"

Bringing home the bacon has long meant not only bringing home a desired prize, but doing well and earning a good living.

"buck stops here, The"

President Harry Truman famously had a sign with this slogan on his desk, apparently to describe the finality of the responsibilities of the US government ending in his office. The reverse side said 'I'm from Missouri,' and it was a gift from a friend. The slogan had been in use for a number of years before. Some card games use a marker called a buck. Different players act as dealer. When the **buck is passed** to the next player, the responsibility of dealing is passed. Stopping the buck is to accept the responsibility for dealing. So was Truman accepting responsibility or saying that he was in charge and setting the rules?

"Bug off!"

Bug off is a popular American term which says the same thing as a lot of other definitive sayings. Get lost, make yourself short, make like a tree and leave! It is probably short for the similar British term, 'bugger off!' Its first known American usage was in *The New York Magazine*, February 15, 1971.

> "This time the rapist left with the police. A method I have found personally helpful in discouraging the street molester is to embarrass the hell out of him — that is, turn around and in a loud voice say 'Bug off!'"

The same year it appeared in a slightly different context in *The Best American Short Stories 1971* by Martha Foley:

> "'Well,' Albert Decker said, rising, 'I'll bug off.' No one seemed to object."

"Bummer"

'That's a bummer' is something that I've heard most of my life. But it didn't seem to come into popular usage until the latter part of the twentieth century. A bummer is a situation for which you had highest hopes, yet it flopped.

Perhaps you failed an important test or were not able to go on a much-anticipated trip, or worse, your sweetheart left you for a scum bucket. Now those are real bummers!

"Buying a pig in a poke"

This saying is brought up again in the later saying 'letting the cat out of the bag' (see), and refers to the time when piglets were sold at market in bags. Since a cat was about the size of a young pig, unscrupulous merchants would sometimes defraud the buyer by placing a cat in the bag. Eventually it was no longer prudent to buy a 'pig in a poke.'

Today it is used to refer to buying anything 'sight-unseen.'

"By and by"

Now here's an 'oldie but a goodie.' It means 'after a while' or in the unknown distant future, and has been in use in its present sense since the early sixteenth century, and a form of it for a hundred years before. Originally in the

1400s it meant 'one by one.' It has been used in Christian lore to express hope in eternal life.

"By and large"

How this term came to mean 'on the whole,' or 'generally speaking,' seems strange to me. It was originally a nautical command given to the captain of a sailing vessel, meaning 'sail slightly away from the wind.' There was a danger of being 'taken aback' when sailing too near the wind current.

It is said that it evolved from not wanting to 'sail directly into a statement.' Saying 'by and large' is a way of hedging a direct answer, and speaking in generalities. It is used both in America and Britain.

"By hook or by crook"

Though other origins have been suggested, this old saying is almost certainly to come from a medieval English law stating that peasants could use branches of trees for fire wood if they could reach them and pull them down with their shepherds' crook or their billhook. It had nothing to do with someone being a 'crook.'

The first reference to this is in John Gower's *Confessio Amantis* in 1390.

"What with hepe [hook] and what with croke [crook] they [by false Witness and Perjury] make her maister ofte winne."

Today it is used to mean that something will be obtained by whatever means is necessary, regardless if it is proper or legal.

"By the skin of your teeth"

This popular saying, meaning narrowly escaping disaster, comes from the biblical book of *Job*, chapter *19* verse *20*. The first English translation is from the *Geneva Bible*, 1560, and is a literal rendering of the Hebrew text: "I haue escaped with the skinne of my teethe." Since teeth don't have skin, the phrase is, like many proverbs, metaphorical.

C

"cat's meow, The"

This cute expression meaning 'the ultimate' was first coined by American cartoonist Thomas A. "Tad" Dorgan (1877-1929). He also coined the popular expression, "for crying out loud!" Below is an example of Dorgan's work.

"Cat got your tongue?"

This means, 'What's wrong, can't you say something about this?'

It is believed that this saying has it's origin in the Middle East where thousands of years ago the practice of an eye for an eye was common. It was also customary to punish thieves by cutting off their right hand, and liars by ripping out their tongue. These body parts were fed to the king's pet cats. Ouch!

"Caught red-handed"

Various origins have been given to the expression 'Red-handed,' including an allusion to the culturist symbol of Ulster in Northern Ireland. The term originates very near there, indeed—from Scotland, and refers to having blood on one's hands after committing a murder.

The first use of 'to be taken with red hand' dates back to a usage in the Scottish Acts of Parliament of King James I in 1432. Sir Walter Scott first used the term 'taken red-handed' in his classic novel, *Ivanhoe*. It was long after that before the term became more common as 'caught red- handed.'

Some even claim earlier uses of similar phrases (in their native tongues) by the people of the Indus Valley between 800 and 900 BC, who determined a thief's guilt or innocence by putting the accused person's hands on an axe blade which had been heated until it was glowing red; or the Japanese, who were said to brush the sap from poison ivy on their money, and believed that thieves would break out in a rash and be caught 'red-handed.'

"Caught with one's pants down"

This idiom is similar to 'caught red handed,' but does not necessarily indicate being caught committing a crime.

There is actually a consensus among researchers as to the meaning of this phrase. It means 'to be taken by surprise or caught unprepared.' There are three references as to the possible origin.

The first one, however, seems most likely, and I have chosen it for this book. It relates to the Roman Emperor Caracalla, later known as Marcus Antoninus. He was known as one of the toughest Emperors around 200 BC. Historic legend tells us that while he was on an important journey his armed escort gave him privacy to relieve himself beside the road. A certain Julius Martailis, who had a grudge against the Emperor, took advantage of the opportunity to run forward and kill him with a single stab of the sword. He tried to give chase to the assassin but was killed by an arrow from one of the bodyguards of the now deceased Caracalla.

Hence, 'with your pants down' would conjure up visions of an embarrassed man who was caught at a most inopportune moment.

A related phrase is 'caught with your hand in the cookie jar.'

"chain is only as strong as its weakest link, A"

A proverb which can apply both literally and figuratively, this is often applied to a person who is a member of a group which functions as a whole. In business and family, if one fails to hold up their 'part of the bargain' the purpose is compromised and the whole organism falls apart. It's sort of like 'one bad apple spoils the whole batch' (see).

The phrase dates back to at least the mid-to-late eighteenth century, as it was well established in usage when it was included in Thomas Reid's *Essays on the Intellectual Powers of Man* in 1786.

"In every chain of reasoning, the evidence of the last conclusion can be no greater than that of the weakest link of the chain, whatever may be the strength of the rest."

"Chairman of the Board"

In the late 1700s, many houses consisted of a large room with only one chair. Commonly, a long wide board folded down from the wall, and was used for dining. The 'head of the household' always sat in the chair, while everyone else ate sitting on the floor. Occasionally a guest, who was usually a man, would be invited to sit in this chair during a meal. To sit in the chair meant you were important and in charge. They called the one sitting in the chair the 'chair man.'

Today in business, the head of a corporation is often called the Chairman or 'Chairman of the Board.'

"Chip on one's shoulder"

This one is interesting, because one would not automatically suspect the origin. In fact, there is a bit of a conflict as to exactly when it started. But the US practice could have been a carryover from the English story.

The History of British Work and Labour Relations in the Royal Dockyards, 1999, tells of their eighteenth century practices. The book relates that the standing orders for the Royal Navy Board for August 1739 included the following ruling:

> "Shipwrights to be allowed to bring [chips] on their shoulders near to the dock gates, there to be inspected by officers."

Yes, this mentions chips on shoulders, but not why the saying would be as it is. The American version explains the current usage much better.

You see, in the nineteenth century, there was reportedly a practice in the US of sparring for a fight with a chip on one's shoulder, daring others to knock it off.

Today, 'having a chip on one's shoulder' means that one is carrying a grievance against someone or something. To me it's sorta like daring somebody to knock it off.

"Cleanliness is next to godliness"

This is not from the Bible as some have claimed, or from other ancient Hebrew writings. The first mention seems to have been from the English writer, Francis Bacon, whom some equate with Shakespeare. Though a slight variant, as is often the case with original citations, it is obvious that the meaning is here. In *The Advancement of Learning*, 1605, Bacon wrote:

> "Cleanness of body was ever deemed to proceed from a due reverence to God."

Sir Francis Bacon

Around two hundred years later, John Wesley inferred in one of his sermons that the proverb, as we quote it today, was well-known when he stated:

> "Slovenliness is no part of religion. 'Cleanliness is indeed next to Godliness.'"

"Clean as a whistle"

There is no doubt that this simile has been around for hundreds of years, and likely was originated in the UK. There have been several suggestions ventured by etymologists as to the exact origin and connotation of the phrase.

A version of it was utilized by Robert Burns, the famous bard of Scotland in his poem, *The Author's Ernest Cry and Prayer*. He used the word 'toom' meaning empty, instead of clean.

> "Paint Scotland greetan owre her thrissle; Her mutchkin stoup as toom's a whissle."

Other writers spoke of a pure, clear or dry whistle during this age. The intent however seemed to be that to achieve a pure sound from a whistle, it should be clear or dry. I certainly believe this to be the origin. Later usage turned to 'clean as a whistle.' Some see it as merely the clear, clean tone of a whistle made from a reed.

This became a simile of anything to which this attribute applied.

"Clear as a bell"

A bell is used as a model for clarity because of its unquestionable clear tone.

Its likely origin is from the ads of the Sanora Chime Company, which started manufacturing phonographs in the 1910s. They adopted 'clear as a bell' as their slogan, praising the clear quality of their record players.

"Come hell or high water"

There have been earlier variations of this phrase. The earliest was 'hell *and* high water,' and later, 'through hell and high water.' The first printed examples appeared in the early 1900s and tend to be linked to cattle ranching and herding cattle through tough trails and flooded rivers on the way to market. Go John Wayne!

"Come to Jesus meeting"

Said to have originated in the religious camps on the New Jersey shore in the nineteenth century, this saying today has nothing to do with Jesus, and everything to do with a meeting of the minds. It is a much-used term in Southern America — my 'old stomping grounds' (see). It means something big is going down of which all parties concerned need to be informed and on the same page — a cold hard fact is likely to be revealed and it's probably 'put up or shut up' time.

"Cop or copper"

The old English word 'cop' meant grab or capture, so in the nineteenth century police-men became known as coppers, due to the fact that they were responsible for grabbing or catching criminals. The word 'cop' is actually an acronym for Constible on Patrol.

"Copycat"

This was likely started as a reference to how kittens copy the actions of their mothers. It is an Americanism and first known to appear in print in 1896 in poet S. O. Jewett's highly acclaimed book, *Country of the Pointed Firs*.

> "I ain't heard of a copy-cat this great many years... 'twas a favorite term of my grandmother's."

"Cotton-pickin'"

Well, we Southerners in the good ole US of A know that this sayin' came about from pickin' cotton in the good ole days in 'Miss'ippi' and Alabama. In fact, it was referred to in print in a literal sense in the eighteenth century. But it wasn't until 1942 when a citation appeared as a figurative term, to my knowledge. It is found in a newspaper in a small town in Pennsylvania... (Did I say *PENNSYLVANIA*? Yep!) called *The Daily Currier,* in November 1942.

> "It's just about time some of our Northern meddlers started keeping their cotton-picking fingers out of the South's business."

Not that it hadn't been used in a figurative connotation long before this. Cotton-pickin' or the proper spelling, cotton-picking has always been a contemptuous slang remark. Like 'get your cotton-pickin' hands off of me.' Cotton pickers were originally slaves, and even later, usually of African descent, and it is likely that it was comparing the person to someone which was, unfortunately, not looked upon favorably in that day. But in *my* day I have never conceived it in that respect. I might have said something like, "Wait just a cotton-pickin' minute!" (No disrespect to the particular minute that I was asking someone to wait.) Come to think of it, this was a favorite line of my good friend, Bugs Bunny, whose immortal words ring through all of our minds who were around in that hallowed era:

"Just a cotton-pickin' minute, this don't look like the Coachella Valley to me!"

This term is not used as much in other countries.

"Country mile"

I grew up hearing that some things were 'better by a country mile.' I always thought a country mile must mean a long way. But I walked a lot of places as a kid in the country.

The meaning behind this is derived from the directions people used give in the country. Since, like I did, they walked a lot, a mile was 'just down the road a piece.' When they told you it wasn't but a mile or so, it might turn out to be closer to two miles. So when you were told that something was better by a country mile, it was meant to be a 'heap' better.

In the UK they use a 'Welsh mile,' as Wales is largely rural, and it is nearest to a country mile. So what I want to do in this book is make it unique to phrase dictionaries. I want it to be humorous, and better 'by a country mile.'

"Crack a smile"

The origin for this may not be what you think (see: **Three-in-one explanation**).

"Crazy as a betsy bug"

Unless you grew up in the South, US I mean, you may not have heard this one. But where I was brought up, it was downright common. If someone was uncontrollable, erratic, and irrational, they were 'crazy as a betsy bug.' The expression has been around since the late nineteenth century.

A betsy bug, aka bessie bug, is a member of the Passalidae family of beetles. It is big (about an inch and a half long), black and shiny, and has nasty-looking pincers. It can and will bite people and flies where it wants to. Don't get around one if you can help it, 'cause those things are crazy!

"Cream of the crop"

This has been used for centuries as meaning the very best of anything. It comes from the fact that all old farm boys like myself have known since they were 'knee-high to a grasshopper' (see). When butter is churned, the cream rises to the top of the churn, jar, or whatever it is churned in. I've churned it in both. We used to use gallon milk jars to churn small amounts of the luscious rich stuff. Or if someone wanted a big batch, we used a pottery churn with a wooden dasher which was forced up and down with good old fashioned 'elbow grease'(see).

Cream of the market was an early form of this. The earliest known printed reference to an early form of the phrase, 'cream of the jest' was in John Ray's *Hand-book of Proverbs* in 1670.

Cream of the crop, per se, was probably borrowed from the old French phrase 'crème de la crème,' cream of the cream, meaning the best of the best. It was well-known in English by 1800.

"Crocodile tears"

'Crocodile tears' are an insincere show of grief or sadness. The saying derives from the old wives' tale which said that a crocodile wept insincerely if it killed and ate a person.

"Cut the mustard"

The origin of this phrase is the subject of a long-standing debate among those who research common English euphemisms.

Perhaps the most likely origin is that 'mustard' is a corruption of muster. "Muster' in military vernacular, means to summon troops for inspection. Those who are up to standard are said to have 'passed muster.' Cut normally refers to being able to do something. Therefore to cut the muster would mean to come up to standard.

"Cut to the chase"

This familiar cliché comes from the American film industry, and actually goes back to silent films which often concluded with chase scenes proceeded by romantic storylines. The first preserved reference, though not its original coining, is from the script direction of an early 'talkie,' *Show Girl in Hollywood*, based on Patrick McEvoy's novel *Hollywood Girl*, released in 1930.

"Jannings escapes... Cut to chase."

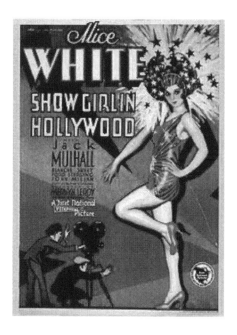

But the figurative usage of the phrase, meaning, 'get to the point,' came considerably later, in the 1940s, and was first printed in a Canadian newspaper. *The Winnipeg Free Press* ran an article in March 1944 about screen-writing which included the following citation:

> "Miss [Helen] Deutsch has another motto, which had to do with the writing of cinematic drama. It also is on the wall where she can't miss seeing it, and it says: 'When in doubt, cut to the chase.'"

Though this implies getting to the point, it still relates to film making. The more general usage comes not long afterward. One example is this line from a piece in the New England newspaper, *The Berkshire Evening Eagle*, in February, 1947:

"Let's cut to the chase. There will be no tax relief this year."

Other similar phrases have emerged, but 'cut to the chase' is still as alive as back then.

D

"Damned if you do and damned if you don't"

Well, I bet you can't guess who originated this. Maybe a gambler?

Nope. A preacher! It was nineteenth century American evangelist Lorenzo Dow.

Dow decided as a young boy to devote his life to 'teaching the word of God' and began preaching when he was only nineteen years old. Although his views were similar to those of the Methodists, he was never formally affiliated with that denomination. He rode on horseback throughout both the North and South of the United States. Dow's dramatic sermons, eccentric manners, and odd-looking clothing made him a frequent topic of controversial conversation. He died in 1834, and in 1836 his written works were edited and published. They included *Reflections on the Love of God*, a strong criticism of preachers who supported the doctrine of Particular Election and confused their congregations by pointing out conflicting statements in the *Bible*. In his writings in a somewhat humorous rhyme,

Dow chastened "those who preach it up, to make the Bible clash and contradict itself, by preaching somewhat like this: 'You can and you can't - You shall and you shan't -You will and you won't - And you will be damned if you do - And you will be damned if you don't.'"

The memorable quote stuck in pop-culture with few people today realizing its true origin.

"Damsel in distress"

This term has come to typify a particular theme of stories, in which a female character is in dire need of rescue by a macho-type male hero. It is based on a French word, demoiselle, which suggests a delicate young woman. The roots of the idea of the 'damsel in distress' go all the way back to Greek tragedies and their harrowing encounters with gods and demi-gods. Naiveté usually characterizes such a fragile feminine character.

A 1919 novel by P.G. Wodehouse bore the title *Damsel in Distress*, and was made into a movie in 1937.

In cartoons, Minnie Mouse was characterized often in this role in the mid twentieth century.

"Dark horse"

Well, this came from the logical circle — the racetrack. A dark horse was one of obscure origins which few people felt had a chance of winning a race. Usually applied after a 'miracle' alters fate. Later it caught on, like all of these animal phrases, and was applied to people.

The earliest known reference was from Benjamin Disraeli in *The Young Duke*, 1831.

> "A dark horse, which had never been thought of ... rushed past the grand stand in sweeping triumph."

The figurative usage of the exact phrase seems to have first been applied to academia in 1865 in Sir Leslie Stephen's *Sketches from Cambridge by a Don*.

> "Every now and then a dark horse is heard of, who is supposed to have done wonders at some obscure small college."

"Dead as a doornail"

It is most likely that the 'door nail' in this idiom refers all the way back to 1350, and was a small metal plate which was nailed onto a door which served as a plate for the knocker. After so many visitors pounded on the 'door nail,' the life would just be pounded out of it, and it would no longer be effective.

Charles Dickens used the phrase in his immortal classic, *A Christmas Carol* to describe the ghost of his old partner.

"Old Marley was as dead as a door-nail."

"Dead to rights"

We've all heard this one. A criminal has been caught 'with his pants down' or his 'hand in the cookie jar.' We think he might as well relinquish his 'rights' and just throw himself on the mercy of the court.

It is certainly a curious expression, and dates back at least to the mid nineteenth century, when a whole heap of these little ditties were hatched up. Or should I hush with the clichés and get down to business? It first appeared in a collection of underworld slang jargon called *Vocabulum, or The Rogue's Lexicon* by George Matsell. The word 'dead' in this phrase was slang to mean 'absolutely, without any doubt.' The use of dead in this respect is more common in England where it dates back to the sixteenth century. It is, of course, accepted in many cases to mean that in the US, like 'for dead sure,' 'dead broke,' etc., etc., etc.

The origin of the usage of 'to rights' here is not so easily pinpointed. Since the sixteenth century it has meant in a proper manner or order. To set to rights, for instance, means to make a situation right. Here it is to mean that every requirement of law has been met. The phrase therefore means that the arrest was clean and justifiable.

"Dead ringer"

This has come to mean someone who looks 'exactly like' another person. You won't believe the origin! (See: **Saved by the bell**)

"Devil-may-care attitude"

Hey, we've all known someone like this. They 'couldn't care less.' They were thought of as careless and reckless, and you told them they took too many risks...that is unless you were this person!

Dictionary.com says 'devil-may-care' has been around since 1785-1795. Merriam Webster says its first known use was in 1837. I found no documentation.

"devil to pay, The"

Originally this old saying was 'the devil to pay and no hot pitch.' In a sailing ship, a devil was the seam between the planks, and it was imperative that it be made waterproof. Fibers from old ropes were hammered into the seam and then a tar-like substance known as pitch was poured (or paid) onto it. If you had the devil to pay and no hot pitch you were in big trouble.

"Dire straits"

A good clue to the origin of this term, believed to have originated in the fifteenth century, is the spelling of 'straits,' which are passageways through which ships navigate. In early years of global exploration and trade growing via ships, navigation through the straits could be very treacherous, and the circumstance would be seen as dire when problems arose. Eventually, waterways were improved, and during normal weather, they are passable.

Now, any time a person is in an especially difficult situation, especially in a financial matter, they are said to be 'in dire straits.'

An eighty's rock band took this for their name.

"Dog-eat-dog"

The Second Edition *Oxford English Dictionary* refers to a quote from 1858 of an old proverb, 'Dog does not eat dog.' The first known printed example of the modern expression is from 1931. It may have been a play on the older saying. It apparently means that the world had by that time become so vicious that a metaphorical dog would indeed eat another metaphorical dog. If that was the case in 1931, then how about the twenty-first century?

The phrase definitely refers to fierce competition, and this is often obvious among dogs fighting over bones or food.

"dog is a man's best friend, A"

This seems to derive from the well-accepted fact that dogs are intrinsically faithful to their owners, and we now know that those with pets are likely to live longer, according to those who do such studies.

The first known publication of this saying is from a poem published in *The New York Literary Journal,* Volume 4, 1821.

> "The faithful dog—why should I strive
> To speak his merits, while they live
> In every breast, and man's best friend
> Does often at his heels attend."

I recently heard that a comedian had stated, "When I die I'd like to come back as a dog in America."

To paraphrase a quote from former British Prime Minister, Harold Macmillan, "Fido, 'you've never had it so good.'"

"Dollars to donuts"

This phrase was meant as 'a sure bet' and was coined in America when a dollar was worth much more than a donut. The apparent first reference I can find is in *The Daily Nevada State Journal,* in February, 1876, which seems rather appropriate now, since Nevada is the state associated most with betting and gaming.

> "Whenever you hear any resident of a community attempting to decry the local paper... it's dollars to doughnuts that such a person is either mad at the editor or is owing the office for subscription or advertising."

Of course, at that date, donut was still spelled the old way, with 'dough' in its full form. And it also seems ironic that 'dough' is a slang way of saying money now. Other similar phrases later sprang up in print like 'dollars to buttons' and 'dollars to cobwebs,' but donuts won out in the hearts of Americans. Maybe because of the fact that it smacks of food, as we all know how much Americans love to eat.

"Don't believe anything you hear and only half of what you see"

Like me, you've probably heard this all your life and didn't know if you should believe it! Well, guess what. It's from Ben Franklin. The actual quote is "Believe none of what you hear and half of what you see." Methinks its pretty good advice, even more so now than back in ole Ben's day.

"Don't bite the hand that feeds you"

Another old one from at least the eighteenth century in England, for political writer, Edmond Burke, used a version of it.

> "...having looked to government for bread, on the very first scarcity they will turn and bite the hand that fed them."

This saying is likely much older, and means exactly what it sounds like. If someone is being kind to you, return the kindness, don't fight them.

"Don't count your chickens before they are hatched"

Surprisingly to me, this tidbit of wisdom is one of the oldest of this type of sayings. It was first recorded in Aesop's fable from 570 B.C. entitled *The Milkmaid and Her Pail*.

> "A milkmaid was going to market carrying her milk in a pail on her head. As she went along she began calculating what she would do with the money she would get for the milk.
>
> "'I'll buy some fowls from the farmer next door,' said she, 'and they will lay eggs each morning, which I will sell to others. With the money that I get from the sale of these eggs, I'll buy a new dress for myself. This way, when I go to market, all the young men will come up and speak to me! Other girls will be jealous but I won't care. I will just look at them and toss my head like this.'
>
> "And with those words, the milkmaid tossed her head back. The pail fell off her

head and all the milk was spilled on the ground. She had no choice but to go home and tell her mother what had happened to the milk.

"'Ah, my child,' said the mother, 'do not count your chickens before they are hatched.'"

It was much later used by Thomas Howell *in New Sonnets and Pretty Pamphlets* in 1570. Obvious is the intent—don't be so quick to count on something that may not materialize, particularly financial gain.

"Counte not thy Chickens that vnhatched be,
Waye wordes as winde, till thou finde certaintee."

A little later there is a reference used by Samuel Butler in his narrative poem, *Hudibras* in 1664.

"To swallow gudgeons ere they're catch'd,
And count their chickens ere they're hatched."

"Don't cry over spilt milk"

This saying means not to worry over unfortunate events which have already happened, and which you are unable to change.

This proverb has roots so deep that it's impossible to dig them all up. Researchers believe that it likely originated with folk lore about fairies. In the ancient world it was thought that laying out a 'shrine' with food for fairies would bring good fortune to a house. Needless wasting food added difficulty to feeding the family. However, when milk was spilled, if someone pined over it, it was considered that they were unwilling to give the gift to the fairies, so crying over the loss was scolded.

The earliest reference I have found is from England, in 1659, in *Paramoigraphy* by James Howell, brother of the Lord Bishop of Bristol:

"No weeping for shed milk."

"Don't have a pot to pee in or a window to throw it out of"

In medieval London, at the time this was coined, there was no indoor plumbing, and chamber pots were the common toilets. At that time, many people dumped them out their windows into the gutters beside the streets below. Even the very poor had these pots, so saying this was taking a person to the lowest rung of poverty.

Some areas of the world and some Amish communities still use chamber pots today.

"Don't look a gift horse in the mouth"

This proverb comes from the fact that by examining a horse's mouth, a person who knows the scoop on horses can tell their age. Their teeth project a bit more forward each year. This phrase means 'don't examine too carefully the motives of a person who is making a gift to you without asking for something in return, or try to examine its worth before accepting it gratefully.'

This is an ancient saying of obscure origin which goes back to at least the sixteenth century. The first known printing of a similar proverb was 'Don't look a given horse in the mouth' in John Heywood's 1546 work, *a dialogue conteinyng a nomber in effect of all the prouerbes in the Englishe tongue.*

"No man ought to looke a geuen hors in the mouth."

Heywood's work is the source of early printings of many sayings. He was employed in the court of King Henry VIII and Mary I as a musician and playwright. His proverbs rank only second to those of the *Bible* in historic significance, it seems. (See others in this book.)

"Don't kill the goose that lays the golden eggs"

(See '**Your goose is cooked.**')

"Do unto others as you would have them do unto you"

Upon this proverb many religions have built their philosophy. It is one of the oldest sayings known to man. This particular version comes from the words of Jesus in *Matthew 7:12*.

It first appeared in English in 1535 in the *Miles Coverdale Bible*.

"Therfore what soeuer ye wolde that men shulde do to you, eue so do ye to them."

In various forms, the principle expressed in this proverb is conveyed in the classic literature of ancient Greece, Rome and the holy writings of Islam, Taoism, Sikh and other religious texts.

It is universally known as the 'Golden Rule' and various businesses have adapted the name. Some use it as a slogan. A popular colloquial form is 'do as you would be done by.'

"Don't throw the baby out with the bath water"

This old idiomatic expression means that in attempting to get rid of something bad we should not also illuminate the good along with it. It came from the German proverb, 'das Kind mit dem Bade ausschütten.' The first printed record of this phrase is in *Narrenbeschwörung* (*Appeal to Fools*) by Thomas Murner in 1512. This proverb was common in past centuries in German, and was used in the writings of such notables Martin Luther, Johann Wolfgang von Goethe, Otto von Bismarck, Thomas Mann and Gunter Grass according to David Wilton in *Word Myths, Debunking Urban Legends*.

Thomas Carlyle utilized this idea in his essay on slavery titled *Occasional Discourse on the Negro Question* in 1849, admonishing slave owners to end slavery while retaining the dignity of the slaves:

> "And if true, it is important for us, in reference to this Negro Question and some others. The Germans say, 'you must empty-out the bathing-tub, but not the baby along with it.' Fling-out your dirty water with all zeal, and set it careering down the kennels; but try if you can keep the little child."

"Drunk as a skunk"

We obviously know that this phrase has nothing to do with the lovable, yet oft avoided furry mammal. The phrase is simply one derived from the habit of rhyming our sayings.

Though similar expressions in the English language date to the fifteenth century, 'drunk as a skunk' dates only to the twentieth century.

"Dyed in the wool"

Anciently, this was originated by wool that was dyed before it was woven, because it kept the dyed color better than woolen cloth which was dyed after the weaving.

The first example of figurative use, unchanging in purpose and belief, appeared in *The Friend, a Religious and Literary Journal*, March 10, 1910:

> "But the Mojaves have ever been dyed-in-the-wool pagans, and are not very promising material to work with."

E

"Early to bed and early to rise makes a man healthy, wealthy and wise"

It's difficult for anyone my age not to recognize this proverb as coming from Benjamin Franklin in *Poor Richard's Almanac*. I just thought I'd throw it in for the 'young whippersnappers' (see) wondering why most of our generation believed this stuff.

"Earmark"

The use of the term 'earmark' for designating something for a specific purpose came from the days when cattle and other livestock had their ears marked so that their owner could be identified. Even in modern times some ranchers use tags on the ears of cattle to identify them in the stock sales.

"Easy come, easy go"

I was unable to find an exact date of origin, This old axiom, often applied to money and the things it can buy, and indicating no concern over them. It gained great popularity in the twentieth century, particularly in the US.

Originally the title of a 1928 film starring Richard Dix, it was also the title of a 1967 movie starring Elvis Presley and the title song from it, plus a number of other songs through the years, including ones by Bobby Sherman and country superstar, George Straight.

"Eat humble pie"

The original expression was to eat umble pie. Umbles were the intestines, or less desirable parts of an animal. Servants and low-class people ate these parts of animals. If a deer was killed on a hunt, the rich ate the tasty venison, while their servants ate umble pie. In time the phrase became corrupted to 'eat humble pie,' and came to signify debasing oneself or acting with humility.

"Eat out of house and home"

I was told that this was what some people did who visited a while too long. After all, 'fish and company stink after three days' (see).

Most folks would never realize that this is another phrase of Shakespearean origin. If comes from *Henry IV, Part II*, 1597.

> "Mistress quickly:
>> 'It is more than for some, my lord, it is for all, all I have. He hath eaten me out of house and home; he hath put all of my substance in that fat belly of his, but I will have some of it out again, or I will ride thee o' nights like the mare.'"

"Elbow grease"

According to *B.E.'s New Dictionary of the Terms Ancient and Modern of the Canting Crew*, published about 1698, 'Elbow grease has been a term of hard manual labor since 1639.'

I knew all of my youth that it was something to be applied to the cleaning of farm equipment and polishing shoes.

"Every cloud has a silver lining"

The thought behind this positive proverb was given graciously to us by the classic poet, John Milton in *Comus: A Mask Presented at Ludlow Castle* in 1634.

> "I see ye visibly, and now believe
> That he, the Supreme Good, to whom all things ill
> Are but as slavish officers of vengeance,
> Would send a glistering guardian, if need were
> To keep my life and honour unassailed.
> Was I deceived, or did a sable cloud
> Turn forth her silver lining on the night?
> I did not err; there does a sable cloud
> Turn forth her silver lining on the night,
> And casts a gleam over this tufted grove."

Clouds with silver linings appear frequently in literature after Milton's day, usually calling them 'Milton's clouds.' But not until Victorian days did it begin to be quoted as a proverb.

In 1840, the first such reference appeared in *The Dublin Magazine, Volume 1*, in review of the novel, *Marian; or, A Young Maid's Fortunes*, published that year by Mrs. S. Hall.

"As Katty Macane has it, "there's a silver lining to every cloud that sails about the heavens if we could only see it."

Obvious is the fact that the proverb's meaning is that every situation, no matter how hopeless it may seem at the time, shall eventually pass, and that some good result will ultimately prevail.

"Every day of the week and twice on Sunday"

In the South you might ask 'Billy Bob' how often he likes to go fishing, and he could answer, "Every day of the week and twice on Sunday." I heard this so much that I thought it originated in Dixie. 'Taint so.

It goes back to vaudeville days, from the 1880s to the 1930s. Show companies would advertise that they did the show 'every day of the week and twice on Sundays.' Even in the '30s, the shows would only cost a nickel, and it had to be split between the producers, performers, stage hands and everybody, so the more shows they could put on, the more everyone got paid.

F

"Face the music"

Like 'pay the piper' (see), this phrase is referring to owning up to an unpleasant situation; accepting the truth.

It is thought to come from the practice by the old British military of playing the drums when someone was court marshaled. It was said that they were 'drummed out' of their regiment in disgrace.

The first actual reference in writing to the saying, however, was in the *New Hampshire Statesman and State Journal,* in August, 1834.

> "Will the editor of the *Courier* explain this black affair? We want no equivocation — 'face the music' this time."

"Fed up"

This expression dates to the early nineteenth century when the plump gentry in England were compared to farm animals which had been fattened up for market. While the lower class was suffering for want of food, they loathed those who appeared 'fed up.'

The following, from an article in *The Middlesex Currier* in February 1832 speaks of a court case in which it was argued that the Duke of Bourbon couldn't have hanged himself, since he was unable to either stand on a chair or tie a knot. The attorney involved referred to the awkwardness of princes.

> "Every thing being done for them, they never learn to do anything. They are fed up, as it were, in a stall to exist and not act. It is rare to find a Prince who can walk decently across a room."

This phrase caught on, and later in the nineteenth century, other groups of 'idlers' were said to be 'fed up,' and the phrase crept into general parlance. Later usage included 'fed up to the eyeballs,' and 'fed up to the teeth.'

It has since come to be used when anyone has 'had enough.'

"Fight fire with fire"

The roots of this one were passed down to us by Shakespeare in *King John*, 1595.

> "Be stirring as the time; be fire with fire;
> Threaten the threatener and outface the brow
> Of bragging horror."

The origin of the phrase as we know it came from actually fighting fire, when it was done by settlers in the US in the early nineteenth century. In order to put out or prevent additional grass fires, they set small controllable fires called 'back fires.'

In the novel, *A New Home, Who'll Follow, Or Glimpses of Western Life*, by Caroline Kirkland, using the pseudonym, Mrs. Mary Cleavers, based on frontier experiences in Michigan in the late 1840s, we find the following citation:

> "The more experienced of the neighbours declared there was nothing now but to make a 'back-fire!' So home-ward all ran, and set about kindling an opposing serpent which should 'swallow up the rest;' but it proved too late. The flames only reached our stable and haystacks the sooner…"

The earliest known usage of the actual term, 'fight fire with fire,' is American also, and is in Henry Tappan's *A Step from the New World to the Old and Back Again,* 1852.

> "Smoking was universal among the men; generally cigars, not fine Havanas, but made of Dutch tobacco, and to me not very agreeable. I had some Havanas with me, and so I lighted one to make an atmosphere for myself: as the trappers on the prairies fight fire with fire, so I fought tobacco with tobacco."

The phrase came to mean to respond to an attack by combating it with the same or a similar method.

"Fight tooth and nail"

I've seen a few people do this, quite literally. Others do it with words, which hurt almost as badly.

A Latin phrase was the seed of this thought. It was 'dentibus et vnguibus,' literally meaning 'tooth and nail.' In the sense that we know it (as fighting), it appeared in English in 1562 in Ninian Winget's *Certain Tractates*:

"Contending with tuith and nail (as is the prouverb)."

In the sense of 'holding fast,' it is of equal age, and is listed in Erasmus' *Enchiridion Militis Christiani* (another of our frequent sources) in 1533.

"Take and holde this toth and nayle, that to be honour onely which springeth of true virtue."

"Fish and company stink after three days"

This well-used proverb may have been gleaned from 'the wisdom of the ages,' but was passed down to us by ol' Ben Franklin himself, and as 'fish and visitors stink after three days' was included in *Poor Richard's Almanac*.

"Fit as a fiddle"

In the early seventeenth century, when this expression was first coined, 'fit' didn't mean healthy, but rather, 'suitable.' A fiddle, of course, is another name for a violin—one which is still commonly used in bluegrass,

Cajun and country music circles. What folks were saying is that something or someone, in most cases, was suitable for the purpose.

Written 1598, but not published until 1601, William Haughton's comedy play, *Englishmen for my Money*, uses it in the current form:

> "This is excellent ynfayth (in faith), as fit as a fiddle."

Then shortly afterward, in 1603, Thomas Dekker, in *The Bachelor's Banquet*, utilized a slight variation of this phrase.

> "Then comes downe mistresse Nurse as fine as a farthing fiddle in her pettycoate and kertle."

Some say that Haughton's play inaugurated a sub-genre of drama that was exploited and developed by Thomas Dekker and Thomas Middleton over the following years.

Today someone 'fit as a fiddle' is a person in top-notch health who is capable of competing with the best of them.

"Fit to be tied"

This phrase means angry and agitated, and originally referred to putting uncontrollable people in straightjackets, and came into being in the mid nineteenth century.

"Flash in the pan"

This is used of something which offers a lot and delivers nothing. The term has been around since the late seventeenth century, despite attempts to attach its origin to the California gold rush, to which it was applied, and certainly was true. In *Reflections on several of Mr. Dryden's plays,* printed in London, dated 1687, Elkanah Settle wrote these words:

> "If Cannons were so well bred in his Metaphor as only a flash in the Pan, I dare lay an even wager that Mr. Dryden durst venture to Sea."

"Flying by the seat of your pants"

Until the development of the skip/skid indicator near the end of World War I, pilots had no instruments to help them to turn easily and sufficiently. If the aircraft skipped, their bottoms would be sliding 'down hill' in their seats. If they skidded, they would be pushed 'uphill.' Thus the expression came about, "Flying by the seat of your pants." This required heightened awareness. Today this term applies to developing a sense of being able to perform well under less than desirable conditions.

"fly on the wall, A"

I've often wished to be one of these when I was younger — for various reasons. Being 'a fly on the wall' means being able to observe a situation without anyone knowing you are around. Kinda like being invisible. Some people want this so badly that they plant cameras and start scandals. Of course that is illegal, unless you are the CIA, FBI, MI-6, KGB, or something along those lines. Or maybe a production company — better have permission.

This idiom was started in the early twentieth century in the US, and the first known printed reference is from the *Oakland Tribune* (California) in February, 1921.

"I'd just love to be a fly on the wall when
the Right Man comes along."

Nowadays this is used for 'Fly on the wall documentaries' which are filmed of real-life situations supposedly without affecting the day-to-day normal lives of the participants. A type of 'reality show.'

"fool and his money are soon parted, A"

A proverb from the 'wisdom of the ancients,' its thought was well-known by the late sixteenth century when it was brought to light in poetry by Thomas Tusser in *Five Hundreth Pointes of Good Husbandrie* in 1573.

"A foole and his money,
be soone at debate:
which after with sorrow
repents him to late."

This exact wording of the saying is dated at 1587 in Dr. John Bridges' *Defence of the Government of the Church of England.*

"If they pay a penie of two pence more for the reddinesse of them...let them look to that, a foole and his money are soone parted."

This speaks of the folly of putting one's entire hope and effort into obtaining money and the things it will buy, while leaving out love of family and faith in God, as outlined in the Bible stories of rich men who demanded more and more and died, taking nothing with them.

"Footloose and fancy free"

This term came into usage, as I recall, in the latter half of the twentieth century referring to someone who is unattached romantically and free to do whatever they want without fear of retribution.

The word 'footloose' has been around since at least 1863, as it was listed in the *Oxford Dictionary* at that publication. It is noted as having its origin in the US.

The idea of 'fancy free' is believed to have come from loose-footed snails on which 'the re-straining ropes at the base have been slackened off,' according to *"The Phrase Finder"* web site.

"Freelance"

Now used primarily of writers or reporters who work on their own under contract, this saying had its genesis in the Middle Ages. 'Freelances' were Italian and French knights who fought for whomever would hire them: for good or bad. They were literally free lances. But the term didn't originate then, but with Sir Walter Scott as 'free lance' in his classic novel, *Ivanhoe* in 1820.

Sir Walter Scott

"friend in need is a friend in deed, A"

This is another of the oldest proverbs known to man. The principle was stated in writing as early as the third century BC. Famed Roman Era writer, Quintus Ennius wrote, "Amicu certus in re incerta cernitur." The literal translation from the Latin is "A sure friend is known when in difficulty."

The Oxford Dictionary of Quotations lists it as existing in the English language from the eleventh century, but the earliest verifiable reference is from William Caxton's translation of *Four Sonnes of Aymon*, 1489.

"It is sayd, that at the need the friende is knowen."

Then, in the sixteenth century, like so many others, it was recorded by John Heywood, this one in *A Dialogue Conteynyng Prouerbes and Epigrammes*, 1562.

"Prove thy friend ere thou have need; but, in deed.

"A friend is never known till a man have need."

G

"Get the kinks out"

Kink is a Dutch word meaning twist, as the twists in a knotted-up rope. Kinks are considered anything that causes confusion or obstruction. This saying is from the seventeenth century, and fits all connotations, whether mental, emotional or physical.

"Getting the short end of the stick"

This saying goes all the way back to medieval Europe, and a technique known as the 'split tally' used to record money exchange (at the time, coins) and debts. The fund was regularly short, and a squared stick was used which was marked with notches and split lengthwise. Each party was given one of the equal halves to record the debt and had proof of the amount according to the number of notches. Later, this method was altered in order to prevent tampering.

One refinement was to make the two parts of the stick of different lengths. The longer part was called 'stock' and was given to the party which had advanced money to the receiver. This is actually the origin of the word 'stockholder.' The debtor, on the other hand, "got the short end of the stick."

Today 'getting the short end of the stick' indicates getting the bad end of a deal in any type of transaction.

"Getting up on the wrong side of the bed"

This is a superstition which can be traced all the way back to the Roman Empire, when it was claimed the wrong side of the bed was the left side. People have been saying that other folks got up on the wrong side of the bed for well over three centuries now to indicate that they got up in a bad mood, and I don't think any of them knew where the origin of 'wrong side of the bed' actually came from. There is another saying, 'got up with their left foot forward' that might give a hint of this. A lot of English superstitions resulted from the inferiority of the left from the right, which is even older than Rome. One says that it is bad luck to put your left shoe on first. It is said that

Augustus Caesar was very particular to arise each and every morning on the right side of the bed.

As long as three thousand years or more ago, left handed persons were looked down upon as being inferior — something that southpaws are often up-in-arms about. Consider the fact that Alexander the Great, Julius Caesar, Napoleon, Michelangelo, Leonardo da Vinci, Beethoven, Benjamin Franklin, Mark Twain, Albert Einstein, Paul McCartney, Bruce Jenner, John McEnroe, and Bill Clinton were all born left-handed. Need I say more?

"Give someone the cold shoulder"

In days of yore, when an unwanted visitor came, the host would give them a cold shoulder of mutton instead of hot meat as a hint that they should not call again.

The first printed reference to the phrase is in Sir Walter Scott's *The Antiquary*, 1816.

> "The Countess's dislike didna gang farther at first than just showing o' the cauld shouther."

Note that the 'cauld shouther' (Scottish dialect for 'cold shoulder') is shown, not eaten.

In a just slightly later work, *St. Ronan's Well*, 1834, Scott also uses the phrase in its current form.

"I must tip him the cold shoulder, or he will be pestering me eternally."

As you see in this book, Scott coined several of the clichés we know today.

"God helps those who help themselves"

I want to say something right here about many phrases that people *think* come from the Bible, but don't. This is probably at the top of the list — right up there with 'cleanliness is next to godliness' (see). I have heard people quote 'scripture' all my life that actually came from Shakespeare, Ben Franklin, or some other historic writer. Well, this one is from Franklin, and was included in the 1757 edition of *Poor Richard's Almanac*. In fact, this is thought by many to be the most common of ole Ben's proverbs. And I've certainly found it to be an axiom worthy of thought.

"God willing and the Creeks don't rise."

The old adage "God willing and the Creeks don't rise" originally referred to the Creek Indians and not a stream of water. This phrase was coined by a politician and Congressional Indian diplomat named Benjamin Hawkins in the late eighteenth century. While in the South attempting to negotiate a treaty, Hawkins was requested by President George Washington to return home. In his response, he was said to write, "God willing and the Creeks don't rise." Because he capitalized the word 'Creeks' it is deduced that he was referring to the Creek Indians.

"Go fly a kite"

The idea of telling someone to go fly a kite came from colonial America, and the idea that Ben Franklin discovered electricity while flying a kite. Telling someone to go fly a kite was originally intended to be a way of telling someone to go find a better idea—make a new discovery. It has come to mean, 'get lost' or 'make yourself scarce.'

On the Origin of the Clichés & Evolution of Idioms

"Going to hell in a handbasket"

Hey, I've heard this said many times about the deteriorating condition of lots of things — society, the country, politics, and on and on. But where and when did it originate?

Sure enough, it started in America — but not in the twenty-first century, or even the latter twentieth century. It was coined way back in the *early* twentieth century. So what's a handbasket? It's just a basket with a handle. Whatever is being carried in one goes wherever it is being taken with no resistance.

James Rader, an editor with Merriam Webster writes in *The Dictionary of American Regional English* that the saying 'to go to heaven in a handbasket' was recorded much earlier than 'to go to hell in a handbasket' which he indicates appears to have come about in the 1950s. Because of a reference to 'head in a handbasket' from Samuel's diary in 1714, Mr. Rader presumed that the saying could have been around 'much longer than our records indicate.'

"Go jump in the lake"

Like 'go fly a kite,' this cliché was used freely in the mid nineteenth century to ask someone to 'bug off.' It originated in the US. Unlike the other saying, this one gave no hint of finding a 'better mousetrap.' As the years passed, it became outdated by less flattering ways to say the same thing.

"Goodbye"

Most people today have probably never given a thought to the origin of this everyday expression used at parting. However, this was originally a contraction of the words 'God be with ye.'

"Good Samaritan"

We are constantly hearing news stories in which some 'Good Samaritan' is heralded for saving a life of rescuing some poor 'damsel in distress' (see) from a horrible fate.

The original 'Good Samaritan' is from a parable in the *Bible* (*Luke 10:25-37*), when Jesus was using the example that often the person who does the right thing is not the one whom we would expect to do so. The story goes that a certain Jewish man was beaten and robbed (we might say 'mugged') and left by the road for dead. A priest and a Temple worker came by, and went across the street to avoid helping. You might say 'they didn't want to get involved.'

Then a mixed-race man from a group against whom the Jews had great prejudice saw the injured man and took mercy on him, treated his wounds and took him to the 'hotel' and put him up, and offered to pay any cost of caring for him until he was well. Jesus said this man, not the 'holier than thou' (see) Jews was the one who was doing right.

"Goody-two-shoes"

We've all heard someone called this in a brush of sarcasm by someone who felt the other individual was trying to pretend to be saintly when in fact they were far from it.

This idiom comes from the title of a long-forgotten anonymous 'Cinderella-type' tale published in 1765, *The History of Little Goody Two-Shoes*, sometimes accredited to Oliver

Goldsmith due to style and period. The book was intended to illustrate the Christian teaching that diligence reaps its reward in the next life.

'Goody Two-Shoes' is the handle ascribed to a poor orphan girl named Margery Meanwell. She is so terribly impoverished that she only owns one shoe. When a rich gentleman bestows her with a pair of shoes, she keeps repeating that she has two shoes.

> "She ran out to Mrs. Smith as soon as they were put on, and stroking down her ragged Apron thus, cried out, 'Two Shoes, Mame, see two Shoes.' And so she behaved to all the People she met, and by that Means obtained the Name of 'Goody Two-Shoes.'"

Little Goody Two Shoes.

This gift placed within her the desire to press forward, so she worked very hard and eventually married a wealthy widower.

From the turn of the twentieth century, people considered self-righteous have been dubbed 'Goody-goody,' which eventually gave way to 'Goody Two-Shoes.'

"Got my goat"

Getting someone's goat is getting up their 'ire.'

I keep asking myself how all these animals got into our English idioms. What's a goat got to do with getting upset about something?

For the answer to this, we turn to a little American book, written under the pseudonym, "Number 1500" published in 1904 called *Life in Sing Sing*. Therein the word 'goat' is given as slang for anger.

The first mention of the phrase, per se, seems to be from a Wisconsin newspaper called *The Stevens Point Daily Journal* in May of 1909.

"Wouldn't that get your goat? We'd been transferring the same water all night from the tub to the bowl and back again."

It made its way across the pond to England by at least 1924, when it was used in a story by Nobel Prize winner John Galsworthy called *White Monkey*, clearly seen as a recently coined expression.

"That had got the chairman's goat! – Got his goat? What expressions they used nowadays!"

"Go to pot"

We think of this term as going bad, downhill, or to ruin. In past centuries, any farm animal that had outlived its usefulness, such as a cow which could not bear calves and give milk, or a hen that no longer laid eggs, would literally go to the owner's pot. It was cooked and eaten.

"Gossip"

Early politicians needed feedback from the public to determine which issues people deemed important. Since there were no media devices, such as telephones, televisions or radios, the politicians sent their assistants to local taverns, pubs, and bars, telling them to 'go sip' some ale and listen to people's conversations and political concerns. The two words 'go sip' were eventually combined when referring to local opinion and, thus the term 'gossip.'

"Grasp at straws"

Grabbing or grasping at straws is a term which has been around since the mid eighteenth century to mean a desperate and almost certainly futile attempt to save oneself in a time of great adversity. The term lives on.

The first known reference in print to this adage is in Samuel Richardson's lengthy novel, *Clarissa*, in 1748.

"A drowning man will catch a straw."

The meaning was derived from the fact that reeds which grew by the sides of rivers were hollow, and if a man who was being pulled down by the current could grasp one, he may be able to breathe through it as he went under, helping him to survive until he could paddle ashore.

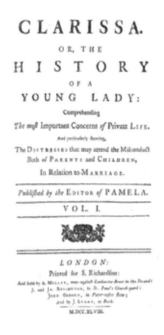

Clarissa is the longest real novel in the English language, consisting of 969,000 words.

"grass is always greener on the other side of the fence, The"

This is certainly a metaphoric proverb, and one of the most widely used sayings in the English language. It speaks of the urge of humanity to be dissatisfied and always look for something they don't have. It's what makes us want to 'keep up with the Joneses'(see).

This idea was expressed in the Latin proverb, "Fertilior seges est alieno semper in arvo," used by Erasmus of Rotterdam and translated by Richard Taverner in 1545 as "The corne in an other mans ground semeth euer more fertyll and plentifull then doth oure owne." Having gained a bit of notoriety in the sixteenth and seventeenth centuries, this earlier version never quite caught on in the main stream of British culture, but certainly seems to me to be the source of the current proverb. In 1959 a play debuted by Hugh and Margaret Williams titled *The Grass is Always Greener,* with the variant, 'on the other side of the hedge.' Other mid nineteenth century variants are 'Distant pastures always look greener,' and 'Cows prefer the grass on the other side of the fence.'

"Graveyard shift"

I have never worked for a factory or other company with around-the-clock production, so I have missed the 'pleasure' of working on the graveyard shift. But millions of people have had that honor.

The origin of this expression actually had nothing to do with graveyards or burying people. Back in the old days, when sailors and ocean-faring folks went to sea, those who worked the late night hours got blurry-eyed, and their eyes watered trying to stay awake. Since any thick liquid was called 'gravy' the saying 'gravy-eyed' came to be among sailors. The late-night shift was then called 'the gravy-eyed shift.' When the sailors were in at port and went into pubs, they told others that they were pulling 'the gravy-eyed shift.' Land lubbers somehow didn't get the phrase, and among themselves, thinking in the super-stitious notions of the era, began calling it the 'graveyard shift,' believing it to be a late-night watch for the dead spirits, or something of that sort. Evidently, the imagined phrase caught on, for this is what it is still called today.

"Green with envy"

The more I get into these idioms, the more I realize what a tremendous influence the plays of Shakespeare had on our modern concept-tions of the English language. Before Shake-speare, the color 'green' brought to mind other emotions than envy and jealousy, such as fear, ill-humor and illness. But he changed it all with the flick of a quill.

In a famous passage Iago warns Othello to 'beware, my lord, of jealousy; /It is the green-eyed monster which doth mock/The meat it feeds on' (*Othello*, III, 3, lines 169-171). This was obviously derived from a green-eyed cat playing with a mouse victim.

"Grin and bear it"

This means to accept an unpleasant situation when there is nothing we can do to change it.

Since I can find no older reference I must assume that this saying is based on a daily syndicated cartoon which was started in 1932 by George Lichty, until 1940, and others from 1942 to the present. After Lichty, it was continued by Fred Wagner, Rick Yager and Ralph Dunnigan. Lichty's style has carried over in the works of various cartoonists in other popular strips.

H

"handwriting is on the wall, The"

It is recorded in the *Bible*, in *Daniel chapter 5*, that when Belshazzar had replaced his father, Nebuchadnezzar, as King of ancient Babylon, he prepared a great feast for a thousand of his lords. At the feast, he became intoxicated and he and his wives and concubines and lords drank from the sacred vessels of the Temple in Jerusalem, and praised their gods.

Suddenly, the finger of a man's hand appeared and wrote four foreign words on the wall of the palace, *'mene, mene, tekel, upharsin.'*

When this happened, the king went into panic, and he ordered his servants to bring the fortune tellers and anyone who might be able to interpret these words, promising that anyone able to do so would be given great gifts and prominence in his kingdom. No one brought had a clue to the meaning of the writing. Then the queen told him that a prophet in his kingdom had 'the spirit of the holy gods' in him, and had interpreted dreams for his father, so he sent for him. His Hebrew name was Daniel, but Nebuchadnezzar had named him Belteshazzar. So the king called for Daniel.

Daniel told the king that he did not want his gifts, but he would interpret the writing for him. He told Belshazzar that there was but one God, and He had given the kingdom to his father, Nebuchadnezzar, who had miserably failed and had become insane like a wild animal. Now, Belshazzar had also failed as king, and gone after heathen gods. As a result, 'the writing was on the wall.' Paraphrased, the words meant, 'God has measured your days as king and you have been weighed in the balance (or scale) and found wanting,' or 'come up on the short end of the stick' (see) so to speak.

If it is said that 'the handwriting is on the wall' today, it means that there are clear signs that something or someone is surely doomed to fail.

"Head over heels"

Now here is a curious phrase which everyone has heard that has come to change in meaning through the years. We often think of it as being 'head over heels in love.'

When the phrase was originally coined it meant something was upside down, or 'topsy-turvy.' It came from flipping 'head-over-heals' when turning cartwheels, which seems like the opposite to me. The first known reference to this phrase is in Herbert Lawrence's *Contemplative Man* in 1771.

> "He gave [him] such a violent involuntary kick in the Face, as drove him Head over Heels."

Love wasn't brought into the equation until 1834, when the legendary American frontiersman and Congressman, David Crockett, used it in his personal memoirs, *Narrative of the life of David Crockett*, 1834.

> "I soon found myself head over heels in love with this girl."

I always perk up a bit when old 'Davy' is brought up, since I share something with him other than living in the state of Tennessee — the anniversary of our birth on 17 August.

Head over heels after this came to mean 'all shook up' over something. Overwhelmed, so to speak, by something exciting — particularly love.

"Heard it through the grapevine"

After the invention of the telegraph in 1844, it became clear that the rural communities already had a pretty effective system of communications through the mouth-to-mouth method. A saying developed that it was a 'grapevine telegraph' — a humorous allusion to the fact that grapevines were the nearest thing to wires in those areas.

In 1876, *The Reno Daily Gazette* ran an article about the bumper corn and grape crops that year. They commented on the fact that the people then known as 'Indians and Negroes' seemed to already be aware of it. (Did they not imagine that they were likely the ones who had done the labor of harvesting the crops?)

> "It would seem that the Indians have some mysterious means of conveying the news, like the famous grapevine telegraph of the negroes in the [American Civil] war. The Pioneer Press and Tribune says that, while the first telegraphic news of Custer's death reached them at midnight, the Indians loafing about town were inquiring about it at noon."

Hearing news through the grapevine came to mean from an informal contact or spread mouth-to-mouth by those who are free to repeat gossip. Like so many clichés, it became the title of a hit song—first released by Smokey Robinson in 1967 and soon after by Gladys Knight and the Pips. Later it became a signature song in 1968 for Marvin Gaye, who actually recorded it before Gladys Knight. In 1970 it was also released by CCR (Creedence Clearwater Revival).

"Heavens to Betsy!"

When I was growing up in the American South, this saying was still fairly common. It was an exclamation of surprise, like 'my goodness!' or 'gracious sakes,' and all are rather archaic now. It originated in America in the mid-to-latter nineteenth century, and was mostly restricted to the US. It faded to near oblivion during the twentieth century. The first known example is from *Ballou's dollar monthly magazine Volume 5*, January 1857.

"'Heavens to Betsy,' he exclaims…"

It is likely that the saying just evolved, and did not apply to any particular 'Betsy.' In 1955 etymologist Charles E. Funk published a collection of phrases entitled *Heavens to Betsy!*

& other curious sayings. Therein he concluded that the actual origin of this phrase was 'completely unsolvable.' Strange conclusion, when this was the book's title.

"Heavens to Murgatroyd!"

This is a variant of the previous exclamation, 'heavens to Betsy!' Those who were around in the 1960s remember that it was made popular by a cartoon character called 'Snagglepuss.'

But the lovable cat with a lisp didn't start it. It was first uttered by Bert Lahr, later famous for his role as the cowardly lion in *The Wizard of Oz*, in the later 1944 film, *Meet the People*. The voice of Snagglepuss was actually patterned after Bert Lahr's voice as the unforgettable big cat in *Oz*, and the saying, 'heavens to Murgatroyd' borrowed from *Meet the People*.

Though there is no definitive origin for this particular 'Murgatroyd,' it has a long-standing place as a surname in British aristocracy. Likely these nobles are the source for a number of Baronets in Gilbert and Sullivan plays with this name in the late nineteenth century and the likely reason for the use of 'Murgatroyd' in this exclamatory saying.

"High as a kite"

High as a kite is seldom used with 'as' at the beginning, hence it goes here in the alphabetical order of things.

'High' has been used in the sense of intoxication since the 1600s, and this phrase has been around since the early 1900s. This is now used for any form of 'being high,' whether caused by alcohol or drugs.

"Hit the nail on the head"

This phrase is so old that its exact origin is lost in obscurity. The earliest known surviving autobiography in the English language, *The Book of Margery Kempe*, written in 1436, and not published for five hundred years, makes reference to this saying.

> "Yyf I here any mor thes materys rehersyd, I xal so smytyn ye nayl on ye hed that it schal schamyn alle hyr mayntenowrys."

The modern English equivalent is:

"If I hear any more these matters repeated, I shall so smite the nail on the head that it shall shame all her supporters."

Still, this hardly does justice to the current meaning and usage of this common idiom. It means that one has stated or done something exactly in the proper manner.

The first citation which appears to 'hit the nail on the head' as to its current usage is from William Cunningham's great scientific work, *The Cosmographical Glasse* in 1559. It speaks for itself as to the knowledge of the phrase in that era.

"You hit the naile on the head (as the saying is)."

"Holier than thou"

This is just what it sounds like: an expression from the *Bible*. In *Isaiah 65:5*, the Old Testament prophet condemns people who say 'stand by thyself, come not near me for I am holier than thou' (KJV).

"Honeymoon"

Traditionally the word moon has been used for 'month' by native tribes in various lands, because of the complete changes of the moon each 30 days. It is no different here. The word honeymoon originally meant 'honey month' in ancient Britain, where the newly-married couple was to drink mead, made with honey, for a full month after the wedding in celebration.

"Honor among thieves"

I would not have imagined that this saying has been around as long as it has. It seems to have originated in English. *The Oxford Dictionary of Proverbs* tells us the concept is found in circa 1622–1623 and cites *Soddered Citizen,* which I learned was a comedy play by Maramion Redux, preformed by the King's Men at Blackfriar's Theater, likely about 1630.

> "Theeues haue betweene themselues, a truth, And faith, which they keepe firme, by which They doe subsis."

The phrase was close to its modern form by 1802 according *The Works of Jeremy Bentham Volume IV*, page 225, 1843.

"A sort of honour may be found (according to a proverbial saying) even among thieves."

It is in the familiar form, with an addendum, in 1823, according to "J. Bee" in *A Dictionary of the Turf*, page 98.

"'There is honour among thieves, but none among gamblers,' is very well antithetically spoken, but not true in fact.

"Hook, line and sinker"

This common idiom, sometimes 'swallowed (something) hook, line and sinker,' and other times 'fell for (something) hook line and sinker' means to believe something at once without considering its source or testing its authenticity. It is often used to describe how someone thought to be gullible reacts to stories told them by others.

Originating in the United States in the mid-nineteenth century, it is an extension of an earlier English saying, 'to swallow a gudgeon.' A gudgeon is a tiny fish used for bait. The idea implies that the gullible person is like a starved fish which swallows not only the bait, but the entire hook, line and sinker.

"Horse of a different color"

Popular enough to use in the classic movie, *Wizard of Oz* in 1939, the origin of this thought goes all the way back to 1601 and Shakespeare in *Twelfth Night, II, iii.*

> "My purpose is, indeed, a horse of that color."

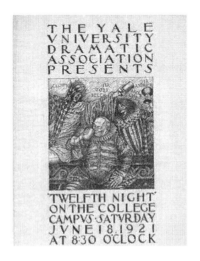

Although this referred to something being of the same matter, rather than a different one, the 'stage was set' and by the end of the eighteenth century, the 'tables were turned,' and it began being used to denote the opposite. For example, in 1798, an article in *The Philadelphia Aurora* used the phrase of President John Adams, sarcastically dubbing him King John I in comparison to the monarch of England, King James I.

> "Whether any of them may be induced... to enter into the pay of King James I is a horse of another color."

"house divided against itself cannot stand, A"

This is another biblical paraphrase that has come into popular contemporary use. It means that any nation, organization, family, club, church, etc., which has a great rift is destined to fall.

> "And Jesus knew their thoughts, and said unto them, Every kingdom divided against itself is brought to desolation, and every city or house divided against itself shall not stand." (*Matthew 12:25, King James Version*)

"How do you like them apples?"

This rhetorical question expresses vexation over some situation. *Random House Dictionary of Popular Phrases and Sayings* says that this has been around since the 1920s, but I can find no documentation of this. Back in the glory days of radio a popular similar phrase was 'How about that?' used by Mel Allen between 1939 and 1964. There is a feeling among researchers that the 'apple' referred to in this 'poor English' saying was a mortar bomb fired by a Stokes gun used in World War I, called 'the toffee apple.'

This line has been popular in movies and on TV. In the Howard Hawks Western film, *Big Sky,* in 1952, starring Kirk Douglas, this is used. In another Howard Hawks Western, *Rio Bravo,* in 1959, Walter Brennan's character, Stubby, throws a hand grenade and says. "How do ya like them apples?" Then, Jack Nicholson's character in *Chinatown,* 1974, says this line. And more recently, Homer Simpson used it in a 1991 *Simpsons* episode and Matt Damon's character in *Good Will Hunting* in 1997.

I

"I could (couldn't) care less"

The original form of this idiom was, of course, 'I couldn't care less,' meaning 'There is no way on God's green earth that I could have the least bit of interest about this subject, so shut up about it! Enough, already!'

The original saying is British, and the first verified reference to "I couldn't care less" is in 1946 as the title for a book by Anthony Phelps. The topic is Phelps' experiences in Air Transport Auxiliary during World War II. It was obvious that the expression was already well-known by that date. It had certainly reached the US during the 1950s, for it was common during those years in my home state of North Carolina. The first time I heard the phrase used in the other sense (I could care less), ironically, was from my twelve-year-old first cousin, Gary Vinson, in 1958. I told him that it was 'I couldn't care less,' and he affirmed his knowledge of the fact and told me sarcastically that he personally had a different version, and he could care less if I, or anyone else, liked it. I wondered later if he hadn't coined it and taken it national, for he entered the military as a teen, and worked with the US rocket program, and later was in a country-rock band. I still entertain the possibility of this, though he is now deceased. From research I have learned that this form *was* coined in the US, and is only found here. It was not found in written form until the 1960s. Strange as it may be, Gary was a leader, a genius, and just may have had the ability to spread his corruption of the phrase to prominence in pop culture.

Attempts to apply logic to 'I could care less' have failed and it is obvious to researchers that the original intent of the change was 'sarcastic.' Way to go, Gary!

"If looks could kill"

Now I would never have suspected that this went back as far as it does. The first known printed reference is from Bram Stoker's *Dracula* in 1897.

> "If ever a face meant death—if looks could kill—we saw it at that moment."

Obviously, this expression is used to express an especially vicious stare intended to convey an unmistakable message of disdain.

"If the shoe fits, wear it"

The roots of this saying go back to England even further than when this first appeared in *The New York Gazette and weekly Mercury* on May 17, 1773 before the US declared its independence.

> "Why should Mr. Vanderbeck apply a general comparison to himself? Let those whom the shoe fits wear it."

The phrase in the old country was 'if the cap fits wear it.' 'If the shoe fits, put it on' is also sometimes used. Recent spins on this proverb include 'If the shoe fits, you're lucky,' a quote from Malcolm Forbes, and 'If the shoe fits, it isn't on sale.' (This is adapted from info found in *Random House Dictionary of Proverbs and Sayings*, Random House, NY, 1996.)

"I'll be a monkey's uncle!"

This saying is derived from a slam against
Darwin's theory of evolution. It means something like, 'Get outta here, I can't believe that!'
Obviously it didn't come into being until after
Charles Darwin's theory was published in *On
the Origin of the Species* in 1859. I have been to
the court house in Dayton, Tennessee where
the famous Scopes Monkey Trial (The State of
Tennessee VS John Thomas Scopes) was held
in 1925 when the high school biology teacher
went on trial for teaching evolution in violation
of Tennessee's Butler Act. Scopes was found
not guilty. This famous trial inspired the
movie, *Inherit the Wind*, starring Spencer Tracy,
Frederick March and Gene Kelley, 1960.

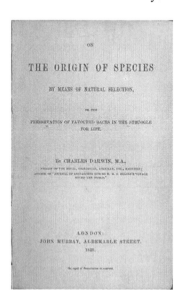

"In a coon's age"

The expression, "I haven't seen you in a coon's age" dates to the nineteenth century, and came about from the belief that raccoons lived a long time. Actually, the life expectance of a well-behaved, healthy raccoon is only from five to seven years. I guess they surmised this because their skin is durable and was good for coon-skin hats and the like back then. The raccoon was the figurehead for the Whig party. They were a bit akin to the modern Republicans who chose the elephant, also having a tough hide.

But I haven't heard this expression in a 'month of Sundays' (see) anyway.

"In a New York minute"

The time and person who first coined this phrase has evidently been lost somewhere on the streets of the city that never sleeps. It likely originated there, but not by a native New Yorker. The saying is derived from the perception that folks in other parts of the country have of New Yorkers—that they have no time for anyone or anything but themselves. Thus a New York minute passes in a flash.

Fortunately, New Yorkers are much like people in other cities — varied in their views, their use of time, and their way of showing their feelings toward others, though they do for the most part live a rushed lifestyle.

The phrase, however, according to the *Oxford English Dictionary,* has been around since the mid twentieth century, and first appeared in print in 1954 (shown below). There was a quote from 1927, but not in the context of the cliché.

> "Betty Jean Bird of the Pirate Club has what she claims the smallest French poodle in the nation...It's no bigger than a New York minute and that's only thirty seconds." *Galveston News* (Texas), 15 August 1954, page 22.

"In high cotton"

I never lived in Alabama or Mississippi, where cotton pickin' was a way of life, even in my younger days. But those who owned the big cotton plantations in the Deep South, particularly in antebellum days, were 'filthy rich,' and those who worked the fields were originally slaves, and later, seasonal or migrant workers. The highest, healthiest plants produced the most cotton. Therefore being 'in high cotton' became a catch-phrase for the envied landowners of the day.

"In like Flynn"

This expression originated in the first half of the twentieth century in America. The popular Hollywood leading man, Erol Flynn, was a real 'ladies' man.' He was suave and debonair. Young men who wanted to be popular with the girls developed the saying 'In like Flynn' to denote that they were able to gain access to a girl's heart.

"In the hood"

This saying became popular in the 1980s referring to the urban neighborhood. Originally it was used as a slang term for a primarily black residential area in the city. Eventually it came to mean the ghetto, or rough parts of town, where gangs form and which many people avoid who don't live there. The term has been used frequently on TV shows and in movies.

"I smell a rat"

Indeed, this happens quite often these days. To 'smell a rat' means something is suspicious; kinda like the Shakespearean quote, "Something is rotten in the state of Denmark" (see).

This goes back, I'm not sure how many centuries, to the time when rats were common pests and carried diseases. Wealthy people would obtain dogs, which had a keen sense of smell, to sniff out the rats and get rid of them. When one of these dogs would perk up his ears and begin sniffing around, it was believed that he 'smelled a rat.'

This came, as many sayings regarding animals have, to be personified.

"It is what it is"

Just thought I would throw this currently popular saying in for good measure, since the first time I heard it was from my good friend, Nate Wolf, in about 2008.

I thought it was a really new phrase when Nate said it relating to a business matter. However, versions of this thought have been around from time in memoriam. One of the first such phrases is found in the biblical book of Exodus, where it is recorded that God told Moses to tell the Israelites that I AM THAT I AM sent you. The name of G-d is so sacred to Orthodox Jewish people that they will not say it aloud. In Hebrew, since there are no vowels, it is spelled YHVH or YHWH.

A clown in Shakespeare's *Twelfth Night* said, "That that is, is."

I was also surprised to learn that this phrase is associated with football and other sports. Live and learn, that's what I say.

"It'll all come out in the wash"

It's sorta surprising how many clichés and proverbs are similar, came from an earlier saying or their meanings overlap. This one is no exception. An earlier version was from *Don Quixote,* by Cervantes, 'all will away in the bucking' (soaking cloth in lye).

Henry Festing Jones, a friend and collaborator with novelist Samuel Butler, quoted him as saying in 1876, "It will all come right in the wash."

"It's all Greek to me"

Now I remember this one from high school Literature class. Like many of the idioms in this book, it came from Shakespeare. It was first spoken by Casca, one of the conspirators against *Julius Caesar* in the first act of the play. He used it in regard to statements made by Cicero after Caesar refused the emperor's crown three times. Cicero had actually spoken in Greek to make sure that the average-Roman-passer-by didn't understand.

The phrase is used to mean that the person speaking has no understanding of what has just been said by a third person.

"It's not over till the fat lady sings"

The precursor of this proverb was 'the carnival isn't over till the fat lady sings.' Its use in sports journalism is attributed to broadcaster Don Cook. His original saying was 'the opera isn't over till the fat lady sings,' shifting the focus of where the fat lady preformed to a more common stage of song. It was first used by Cook in April 1978, after the first basketball game between the San Antonio Spurs and the Washington Bullets, now called the Washington Wizards, during the National Basketball Association playoffs, to illustrate that even though the Spurs had won one game, the series was far from over.

It is said to be derived from the operatic performances which generally feature overweight sopranos at the climax.

The meaning is that we should never assume the outcome of any activity until it is fully played out.

"It's time to pay the piper"

This comes from the sixteenth century tale of the *Pied Piper of Hamelin* (Germany) which inspired the immortal Robert Browning poem in 1842. In 1284, according to the story, the town was infested with pesky rats, and the village people hired the piper to play his pipe and lure the pests away. But when time came to pay the piper, they refused to keep their end of the bargain. He then retaliated, and lured the children away in the same manner.

Just a little lesson — when we agree to a product or service and receive what we request, we must be willing 'to pay the piper.' If we refuse to pay, we must be prepared for the consequences.

J

"Jack of all trades and master of none"

No, Jack is not someone's name, just generic for a common man. The expression, 'Jack of all trades,' which has a negative connotation, goes back to the fourteenth century and an example of this can be found in John Gower's poem *Confessio Amantus* (The Lover's Confession), 1390.

> "Therwhile he hath his fulle packe,
> They seie, 'A good felawe is Jacke.'"

The Oxford English Dictionary defines the medieval name 'Jack' at pretty much the bottom of the social ladder:

> "Jack - A man of the common people; a lad, fellow, chap; especially a low-bred or ill-mannered fellow, a 'knave.'"

Various trades were called 'jacks.' Lumberjacks, steeplejacks, and sailors were called Jacktars. In the Middle Ages, about all trades used the word jack. 'Jack of all trades' was coined as a phrase in 1612. It was then that Geffray

Marshall wrote of his prison experiences in *Essayes and characters of a prison and prisoners.*

> "Some broken Cittizen, who hath plaid Jack of all trades."

'Master of none' was not added until the late eighteenth century. Martin Clifford, headmaster of Charterhouse School, in a collection of notes on the poems of Dryden, about 1677, wrote:

> "Your writings are like a Jack of all Trades Shop, they have Variety, but nothing of value."

Then in 1770, *The Gentlemen's Magazine* included the line:

> "Jack of all trades is seldom good at any."

The earliest known mention of the phrase as we know it today is in Charles Lucas's *Pharmacomastix*, in 1785.

> "The very Druggist, who in all other nations in Europe is but Pharmacopola, a mere drug-merchant, is with us, not only a physician and chirurgeon, but also a Galenic and Chemic apothecary; a seller of druggs, medicines, vertices, oils, paints or

colours poysons, &c. a Jack of all trades, and in truth, master of none."

"Johnny on the spot"

Now here's something my mama wanted me to be pretty often. When she wanted something done, I wasn't to 'lollygag' around 'like dead lice were falling off of me.' I was to be 'front and center' — 'Johnny on the spot!'

The first known printed reference is in *The New York Sun*, in April of 1896.

> "JOHNNY ON THE SPOT. A new phrase has become popular in New York."

Other citations appear around the same time in newspapers and authors' works.

"Jump on the bandwagon"

The word 'bandwagon' was coined in the US in the mid nineteenth century for the wagon that carried a circus band. Circus great, Phineas T. Barnum used the term in his autobiography in 1855, *The Life of P.T. Barnum.*

"At Vicksburg we sold all our land con-
veyances excepting four horses and the
'band wagon.'"

The figurative term, 'getting aboard' or
'jumping on' the bandwagon came later, in the
1890s. Theodore Roosevelt made reference to
this in one of his letters in 1899, which were
published in 1951.

"When I once became sure of one majority
they tumbled over each other to get aboard
the band wagon."

K

"Katy bar the door"

This phrase was in a poem by James Whitcolm Riley published in 1894, but was already in use prior to this time.

When Lide Married Him

When Lide married him – w'y, she had to jes dee-fy

The whole poppilation! - But she never bat an eye!

Her parents begged, and threatened - she must give him up - that he

Wuz jes "a common drunkard!" - And he wuz, appearantly.

Swore they'd chase him off the place Ef he ever showed his face

Long after she'd eloped with him and married him fer shore!

When Lide married him, it wuz "Katy, bar the door!"

It may have come from the traditional Scottish folk song. *Get up and Bar the Door*, published in 1776, in which a stubborn couple were arguing about who should 'bar the door.' However, this poem never uses the name 'Katy.'

Another suggestion is that it originates with Catherine Douglas and her attempt to save the Scottish king, James I. When he was attacked in Perth in 1437, the room he was in had a missing lock bar. The story goes that 'Katy' Douglas tried to save him by baring the door with her arm. The discontented attackers broke her arm and murdered King James. Her story was told by Sir Walter Scott, and afterward the 'lass that barred the door' became known as Kate Barlass, and her descendants still use that name to this day.

"Keep a stiff upper lip"

From the height of the British Empire came the feeling that to do your duty required that you show no emotion. A stiff upper lip indicates such an attitude. This was expressed by Alfred, Lord Tennyson in his famous epic poem, *The*

On the Origin of the Clichés & Evolution of Idioms

Charge of the Light Brigade in 1864 about the famous battle ten years earlier led by the Earl of Cardigan.

> "Forward, the Light Brigade!"
> Was there a man dismay'd?
> Not tho' the soldier knew
> Someone had blunder'd:
> Their's not to make reply,
> Their's not to reason why,
> Their's but to do and die:
> Into the valley of Death
> Rode the six hundred.

Charge of the Light Cavalry Brigade in 1854

Painting by William Simpson

In 1935, P.G. Wodehouse published a novel titled *Stiff Upper Lip, Jeeves.* Pretty British, huh?

But the first printed reference to this phrase is actually American! It was in *The Massachusetts Spy* in Worchester on June 14, 1815.

> "I kept a stiff upper lip, and bought license to sell my goods."

Later printed references are clearer as to the intended meaning of the phrase, however, such as one from the *Huron Reflector* in 1830.

> "I acknowledge that I felt queer about the bows; but I kept a stiff upper lip, and when my turn came, and the Commodore of the P'lice axed [sic] me how I came to be in such company…I felt a little better."

"Keep it under your hat"

This odd-sounding but well-known saying originated at a time when it may have not sounded quite as strange as it does in the twenty-first century. It is recorded in a collection of stories published in London as *The Adventurer* in 1793, on page 309.

> "By a sudden stroke of conjuration, a great quantity of gold might be conveyed under his hat."

It is commonly been told that the conception of hiding items under someone's hat came from the belief that British archers in medieval times used to store spare bowstrings under their hats to keep them dry. But what did this have to do with keeping secrets?

It seems more likely that this referred to keeping the secret in one's head. The earliest known printed reference to this is in *Nuttie's Father*, a novel by Charlotte Mary Yonge, published in 1885.

> "Alice Egremont's loving and unsuspecting heart was so entirely closed against evil thoughts of her husband... while Nuttie, being essentially of a far more shrewd and less confiding nature, was taking in all these revelations... It was all **under her hat**, however, and the elder ladies never thought of her, Alice bringing back the conversation to Mrs. Houghton herself."

Afterward it was utilized by other writers in similar context.

"Keeping up with the Joneses"

This one surprised me a bit. It was inspired by a comic strip by Arthur 'Pop' Momand named 'Keeping up with the Joneses' in the *New York Globe,* first published in 1913. He had originally chosen 'Keeping up with the Smiths,' but changed the title before it was published. By September 1915, a short silent film had been produced by the same name, highlighting women's styles.

Jones, like Smith, was picked as a generic family because it was so common, and the term merely means trying to keep pace in social standing with society around you and others that you may admire and/or idolize.

The idea spawned the E! Reality TV Series which began airing in 2007, *Keeping up with the Kardashians.*

"Keep your chin up"

This is another proverb with American origins. The first known printed reference to this was found in a Pennsylvania newspaper called *The Evening Democrat*, printed in October 1900 in a section on '...the health giving qualities of mirth.'

> "Keep your chin up. Don't take your troubles to bed with you — hang them on a chair with your trousers or drop them in a glass of water with your teeth."

Apparently this section of the paper appealed to those of a certain age who had nothing better to do than to be amused with such stuff...especially considering the reference to 'teeth in a glass.'

"Keep your powder dry"

This idiom means to save your resources until they are needed in order to be prepared for the genuine shortage.

It goes back to the nineteenth century and Oliver Cromwell's campaign in Ireland, when the soldiers had to keep their scarce gun-powder dry and be prepared for battle.

In *Ballads of Ireland*, in 1856, Edward Hayes wrote:

"There is a well-authenticated anecdote of Cromwell. On a certain occasion, when his troops were about crossing a river to attack the enemy, he concluded an address, couched in the usual fanatic terms in use among them, with these words – 'put your trust in God; but mind to keep your powder dry.'"

Wet or wasted gunpowder could have spelled defeat.

Nineteenth century references to this phrase always gave the full context of the original — 'Put your faith in God and keep your powder dry.' It seems that the primary admonishment was that they place faith in God first and foremost, as evidenced in this 1908 article from *The Times Literary Supplement* (London):

"In thus keeping his powder dry the bishop acted most wisely, though he himself ascribes the happy result entirely to observance of the other half of Cromwell's maxim."

"Kick the bucket"

One theory is that an ancient method of slaughtering a hog was hanging it upside down from a beam in a barn designed for this purpose, called a 'bucket.' In its death throes, the porker would naturally 'kick the bucket.'

Another belief is that a method of hanging oneself was to stand on a bucket after placing the noose around the neck, and kick the bucket away. The first theory has more merit. Either seems a bit appalling to me.

"Kill two birds with one stone"

If someone has ever done this in a literal sense, I would certainly like to hear about it. Even killing one bird by throwing a stone would likely be rare.

The intent, of course, is taking care of two needs with a single effort.

Though there were similar phrases used in English and French literature in the sixteenth century, the earliest known printed reference to this cute idiom, as we use it today, was by Thomas Hobbes in *a work on liberty* in 1656.

"T. H. thinks to kill two birds with one stone, and satisfy two arguments with one answer."

"Knee-high to a grasshopper"

Wow, now this is one I well remember. Not because I was short, but because in my childhood, I heard a lot of people say, "I've been doing that since I was knee-high to a grasshopper."

Of course, it means 'little bitty' — either short, young, or both. The saying was one of many metaphoric analogies originating in the nineteenth century. One, 'knee-high to a toad,' may have been used as early as 1814. But the first known record in print of this phrase was from the US Magazine, *The Democratic Review,* in 1851.

"You pretend to be my daddies; some of you who are not knee-high to a grasshopper."

On the Origin of the Clichés & Evolution of Idioms

"Knock on wood"

This expression, related to superstition, is used, usually with the speaker actually knocking on a wooden object such as a table or desk, to ward off bad luck. "I hope that never happens again, knock on wood."

This saying is of ancient origin, and likely related to the worship of trees by various civilizations. Some tribes believed that spirits either dwelt in, or guarded, trees, and these spirits protected the living.

Greeks felt that the oak tree was sacred to Zeus. Celtic peoples believed in tree spirits, and both taught that touching sacred trees would bring good fortune. The Irish folk lore states that touching wood is a way to thank the leprechauns for their luck. Pagan religions had similar beliefs. Both Chinese and Koreans taught that the spirits of mothers who died in childbirth returned to nearby trees.

The wooden cross as a symbol of good luck is actually an adaptation of the older Pagan belief, much like the Christmas tree being brought into the home around the winter solstice.

Perhaps a more direct cause for the current practice is that of the Jewish version. During the Spanish Inquisition, Jews took refuge in synagogues built of wood. To gain admission, they had to know and use a coded knock. Since this practice saved so many lives, it became common practice to 'knock on wood' for good luck.

"Know beans"

A bunch of us have either told someone that they didn't 'know beans,' or had someone tell us that at one time or another.

There was an old riddle which would be told in country stores which went like this: How many blue beans does it take to make seven white beans? The answer was seven. When the seven blue beans are pealed, you have seven white beans. When the person said 'I don't know,' they were told, 'You don't know beans.'

The saying has come to mean that the person doesn't know anything about the subject at hand. I guess if you hadn't heard this before, you just don't know beans.

L

"Lay an egg"

Chickens are expected to lay eggs, but we're not chickens — or we don't want to be. In the early days of playing cricket, it was determined that 'a duck's egg' meant you had no runs. No score was a zero, which looked a lot like an egg. Now we use the term 'goose egg' to mean ZERO.

Today the term 'lay an egg' signifies failure.

"Learn the ropes"

This is a simple one. On sailing vessels it was imperative to learn which ropes were for which purposes and know how to control them. This could prove a life-or-death situation in the event of a storm at sea.

Today it is used to refer to learning the ins and outs of any new business or venture.

"leopard cannot change its spots, A"

The meaning of this proverb is easy to decipher. Someone is what they are by their intrinsic nature. They don't usually change. Although some people really do change, the point is generally well-taken. You shouldn't fall 'hook line and sinker' (see) for someone's story that they have changed until you check their motives, and until they prove themselves.

This is another biblical paraphrase, and is from *Jeremiah 13:23a*.

> "Can the Ethiopian change his skin, or the leopard his spots?"

"Lesser of two evils"

The saying 'the lesser of two evils' is an idea in politics and political science that of two poor choices, one is not as bad as the other.

Originally called 'the lesser evil,' the principle began as a Cold-War-era (between 1946 after the close of WWII, and 1991) pragmatic foreign policy belief utilized by the United States. To a somewhat lesser extent, it was also used by other countries during this time. It dealt with the way third world dictators should be handled.

In our modern world, the idiom is applied to political elections.

"Let's run it up the flagpole and see if anyone salutes"

This catch-phrase, now a cliché, became popular in the US in the mid twentieth century (late 1950s and early '60s) and means 'let us present an idea and see whether it receives enough favorable reaction to proceed.'

Sometimes it is still used humorously with the knowledge that it will be seen as outdated, even by old-timers. It was associated with ad agencies on Madison Avenue in New York, and utilized by comedians poking fun at corporate America, along with such expressions as 'the whole ball of wax' (see).

It was used in the movie *Twelve Angry Men*, starring Henry Fonda, and Stan Freberg's 1961 comedy album, *Stan Freberg Presents the United States of America: The Early Years.*

Allan Sherman used this cliché in his 1963 parody of Gilbert and Sullivan's *When I was a Lad.*

> *I worked real hard for the dear old firm,*
> *I learned most every advertising term.*
> *I said to the men in the dark gray suits,*
> *'Let's run it up the flagpole and see who salutes.'*

"Let the cat out of the bag"

There are two commonly accepted origins for this idiom. The first and most likely is that it came from the days when piglets were sold in markets in bags, and some would put cats in the bags instead. To let the cat out of the bag would expose the fraud. This is also where the saying 'buying a pig in a poke' (see) came from, and is referenced as early as 1530.

Another theory is that the cat referred to a cat o' nine tails which was used to flog unruly sailors in olden days. Though doubtful, this is remotely possible, as there are references to the cat o' nine tails for centuries before any use of letting the cat out of the bag. The nine tails are from the three ends of rope which were each tied off in three more knotted ends. The 'cat' refers to the scratches made by the horrible lashes it cut in the flesh of the victim's back.

"Let your hair down"

I think even the most sophisticated folks still enjoy 'letting their hair down' on occasion. In fact, members of the highest society are the ones who coined this phrase way back as early as the seventeenth century when women's hair was pinned up in elaborate hairdoes. This meant spending hours fixing their hair, and multitudes of hairpins.

It was said that in nineteenth century France during the reign of Napoleon, the women of French nobility would have been fiercely condemned if they had appeared in public without their hair properly pinned. When they returned home, it was quite a relief to take out the pins and 'let their hair down.'

The earliest known reference to the look of women not properly groomed is *John Cotgrave's English treasury of wit and language,* 1655.

"Descheveler, to discheuell; to pull the haire about the eares."

Today, letting one's hair down means relaxing and having a good time — even for bald men!

"Levelheaded"

I thought this expression curious enough to check out how long it had been around. Originally 'level-headed,' it dates back at least to 1876. Another mid-to-late eighteenth century phrase, used to mean sensible and likely to make common-sense decisions. Do you guess the flat-top haircut made guys feel levelheaded in the 1950s and '60s?

"lick and a promise, A"

When I was growing up in the hills of North Carolina, this was a common phrase, especially by the generation older than myself. A lick and a promise meant that the person would do as little as possible now and come back and finish the task when they had more time.

The saying was first recorded in print in 1860, by Walter White in *All round the Wrekin*.

"We only gives the cheap ones a lick and a promise."

"Light at the end of the tunnel"

Most of us know what this means. We have been through dark tunnels along the road of life, and it seemed nice when we finally could discern a glimmer of light at the end of the tunnel. According to the *Random House Dictionary of Popular Proverbs and Sayings*, this expression was first coined around the 1920s, and it was made popular by American President John Fitzgerald Kennedy in the early 1960s in referring to US involvement in the Viet Nam conflict.

"Like a bat out of hell"

If you think this has something to do with bats' supposed connection to blood-sucking vampires getting away from their victims to escape capture, you are *dead* wrong. The bat is essentially a harmless creature.

The phrase 'a bat out of hell' first appeared in print in 1921, but is thought to have been in usage some years longer. It refers to the uncanny speed of a bat in flight, and the 'out of hell' part is likely to have been added for effect, and probably referred to their abode in dark caves. Hades was underground, you know. Others say it may have come from the German word höhle meaning cave. Makes sense to me!

"Like a chicken with its head cut off"

When I've been exceptionally busy, I've often told others that I'd been running around like a chicken with its head cut off. In fact I used the phrase today, and that made me think of it. I've cut a bunch of chickens' heads off growing up on the farm, but none of them ran around afterward. Their nerves did jerk a bit though.

This phrase was known in the United States as early as the late nineteenth century, and appeared in print as a simile by the 1880s. It was used in an article about an escaped prisoner in *The Atlanta Constitution* in July of 1882.

> "Finding himself free from the heavy shackles, he bounced to his feet and commenced darting about like a chicken with its head cut off..."

"little bird told me, A"

This basis of this saying is from the Bible. Solomon wrote in *Ecclesiastes 10:20* that we should not curse the king, or the rich, even in private, or 'a bird of the air' may report what we say.

"little knowledge is a dangerous thing, A"

The two synonymous proverbs, 'a little knowledge is a dangerous thing,' and 'a little learning is a dangerous thing,' have been around since the eighteenth century.

The latter, the original, is attributed to Alexander Pope (1688-1744). It was first printed in *Essay on Criticism*, 1709.

> "A little learning is a dangerous thing; drink deep, or taste not the Pierian spring there shallow droughts intoxicate the brain and drinking largely sobers us again."

In an article in *The monthly miscellany; or Gentleman and Lady's Complete Magazine, Vol. II*, 1774, the writer misquoted Pope, using the word 'knowledge' instead of 'learning':

"Mr. Pope says, very truly, 'A little know-ledge is a dangerous thing.'"

Alexander Pope

Still, it was claimed that Francis Bacon originated the saying earlier. But then did he not also write Shakespeare's plays, according to some? He must have been quite a chap!

"Live the life of Riley"

I haven't heard this one in many years, but I well recall that back in the 1950s it was still very common in the US to mean a life of ease and prosperity.

This phrase, according to some, was popular as far back as the 1880s in England, when the poems of James Whitcomb Riley depicted comforts of prosperous home life. Indeed, he may have been the original 'Riley.' It was spread with the Irish / American soldiers in the US Army during WWI.

The first known published citation is in a letter from a Pvt. Walter J. Kennedy who was stationed at Camp Dix, New Jersey, which was published in *The Syracuse Herald* on June 29th, 1918 under the heading, 'Great Life, Writes Soldier at Camp.'

"This is surely one great life, We call it *the life of Riley*. We are having fine eats, are in a great detachment and the experience one gets is fine."

Later that year *The Bridgeport Telegram* published a letter from Pvt. Samuel S. Polley, who was stationed in France.

"They [German officers] must have led the life of Reilly as we caught them all asleep in beds..."

The phrase reached the wider public via the 1919 song by Howard Pease –

My name is Kelly:

"Faith and my name is Kelly, Michael Kelly, but I'm living the life of Reiley just the same."

"Lock, stock and barrel"

The first known recorded mention of this expression, meaning 'the whole thing' was British from *Major Jones' Courtship* by W.T. Thompson, published in 1842.

"All moved, lock stock and barrel."

The saying is derived from the three parts of a musket, the common gun of that era, a simple devise consisting of a lock, or latch and pin to release for firing, the stock, or stick, a wooden handle used to place against the shoulder when firing, and the cylindrical metal barrel (a name derived from a beer barrel) through which the ball fired.

This book is also the source of the coining of the word 'goatee,' which was adapted from the appearance of a goat's beard.

Through the years the term 'lock, stock and barrel' has came to mean the whole of anything.

"Look what the cat dragged in"

Before the days of pampered pets, when cats actually caught mice in America (I suppose cats may still practice the art of hunting in some parts of the world), it was common for house cats to go out in search of prey, whether mice, chipmunks, birds, or other small, help-less creatures. They had a tendency to proudly drag their find into the house all covered with their saliva, and a bit tattered, and bat it around a few times.

When someone would visit that had not been around for a while, and possibly appeared weather-worn, it became a humorous greeting to remark, "Look what the cat dragged in."

Though the exact origin is unclear, this common saying has been around for 'quite a spell' and is freely used in both the UK and the US.

"Loose lips sink ships"

This idiom, which means 'Be careful what you say, for it may fall upon the wrong ears and be used against you,' was coined during WWII as an American slogan to encourage people to be cautious not to give information to someone who could be an enemy of the country. Originally, it was 'Loose lips *might* sink ships.'

Below is an example found in a Maryland newspaper called simply, *'The News'* and was printed in May, 1942:

> "As countians [attendees at the local county school] registered in the high school lobby before the opening of the meeting, they were surrounded on all sides by placards bearing such admonitions as 'Loose Lips Might Sink Ships,' 'Defense On The Sea Begins On The Shore,' 'Defense In The Field Begins In The Factory' and patriotic creeds and slogans."

Below is a poster used to promote the motto.

"Losing face"

This expression, of course, now refers to doing something which would make you lose your favorable position in the eyes of others. To find the origin of this see: **Three-in-one explanation**.

"Love is blind"

I think this came from my mama when I was 14. Nah, just kidding. But don't you just love it when I tell you one of these little ditties came from Shakespeare or the *Bible*? This one is from old Will Shakespeare. It must have been a favorite line, because he put in several of his plays. Here are a few lines from *Merchant of Venice*.

> "JESSICA: Here, catch this casket; it is worth the pains.
> I am glad 'tis night, you do not look on me,
> For I am much ashamed of my exchange:
> But love is blind and lovers cannot see
> The pretty follies that themselves commit;
> For if they could, Cupid himself would blush
> To see me thus transformed to a boy."

Love really is blind, you know.

"Lying through your teeth"

I wanted to include this phrase so badly that I roamed the Internet looking for sources to determine its origin to no avail. I thought it was curious, however, that one website, answerbag.com, on the page where this was explained, listed ads for attorneys and law schools.

But its meaning seems clear. Lying through one's teeth indicates that the untruth is very intentional. The person speaking is putting on a façade of friendliness and smiling while hiding the wicked truth. It seems that this expression is the same in a number of societies.

M

"Make a mountain out of a molehill"

This oft-used saying refers to making a big deal out of something insignificant. It is one of the most common phrases in the English Language.

The first recorded English usage of the saying was recorded in 1548. Before that, moles were known as 'wand,' later changed to 'want.' A molehill was called a 'want thump.' Later the name for mole was changed to 'moldewamp,' meaning 'earth thrower.' This was shortened to 'molle.'

The idiom is first found in Nicholas Udall's English translation of *The first tome or volume of the Paraphrase of Erasmus vpon the newe testament*, 1548, recorded below:

> "The Sophistes of Grece coulde through their copiousness make an Elephant of a flye, and a mountaine of a mollehill."

It was later recorded in *Foxes Book of Martyrs*, 1570, a book I am proud to have in my library. I could go on and on, but I don't want to make a mountain out of a molehill, now do I.

"man who is his own lawyer has a fool for a client, A"

Obviously uttered the first time by an attorney, whenever that may have been, this proverb first appeared in print in *The flowers of wit, or a chance collection of bon mots,* by Henry Kett, in 1814.

> "...observed the eminent lawyer, I hesitate to pronounce, that every man who is his own lawyer, has a fool for a client."

"Mind your own bee's wax!"

Business, mind your own business, right? For the origin, see: **Three-in-one explanation.**

"Mark my words"

The word 'mark' since the twelfth century has been used by writers and in conversation to mean 'head.' This is a phrase that I heard the generation above me, those born in the early twentieth century, use regularly as I grew up.

The earliest example of "mark my words" I know of is in *Coverdale's 1535 translation of the Bible, Isaiah 28:23:*

> "Take hede, and heare my voyce, pondre and merck my wordes wel." (VSD)

I have heard this both 'mark my words,' and 'mark my word,' but in every case the speaker intended for the hearer to pay close attention, because what he or she was saying was most definitely true, in their opinion, and usually a prediction of something certain to happen because of the chain of events which had already transpired.

"Measure twice, cut once"

This is an old English proverb which dates to at least the late sixteenth century. Its meaning is clear: carefully consider all of the options before making a final decision, especially in important matters, because in some issues, once the choice is made, you won't have another chance to change the course of the matter.

The first reference I have found is in *Second Frutes* by linguist John Florio, tutor at the Court of King James I (compared to and supposed by some to be the real Shakespeare), in 1591:

"Always measure marnie before you cut anie."

Though indecisiveness is often bad policy, this proverb should always be observed. It is like one of my dad's sayings. "Think twice before you speak once." Also wise advice. *(My thanks to my friend Paul Bernhardt for bringing this one to my attention.)*

 **John Florio, 1611**

"Mind your p's and q's"

Various explanations have been given through the years about this expression; including being cautious when drinking alcoholic beverages to distinguish pints from quarts, but the most logical one is that of the printer's apprentice when learning to set type. The lower case p and q were so similar, that the printer would warn the novice in the trade to watch to not confuse them. Hence, 'mind your p's and q's' became synonymous with behaving, not becoming confused and getting one's facts straight.

"miss is good as a mile, A"

When my mother was saying this while I was growing up, I didn't realize that it had been around since the eighteenth century. I just understood its meaning. If I was excited about getting close to hitting something or making a tragic error, it really didn't matter because I had still avoided it.

The first printed example of the proverb as we know it is in a journal called *The American Museum*, Volume 3, 1788.

> "A smart repartee...will carry you through
> with éclat such as 'a miss is as good as a
> mile.'"

But the thought behind it did not originate in
the US. Similar proverbs were in usage in the
British Isles more than a century earlier. The
following, from William Camden's *Remaines of
a Greater Worke Concerning Britaine* was published in 1614.

> "An ynche in a misse is as good as an ell."

It was also present in Scotland in the eighteenth century as a proverb. James Kelley
included it in his publication of *A Complete
Collection of Scottish Proverbs* in 1721.

> "An inch of a miss is as good as a spaw
> (span)."

"Monkey see, monkey do"

'Ain't it th' truth, ain't it th' truth!' Whatever
an adult does, a child will mimic.

*A Dictionary of Catchphrases, American and
British*, lists this as Canadian and American,
originating about 1925. They say that circa 1950

it was adapted to British usage as describing the learning process, and not in the same way as it is used in America.

The Wikipedia article on this phrase claims that it originated in Jamaica in the eighteenth century and 'popped up in the American culture in the early 1920s.' This article further states that the cliché likely originated 'in the folklore of Mali West Africa, well known by Esphyr Slobodkina's retelling, which she calls *Caps for Sale (A Tale of a Peddler, Some Monkeys and Their Monkey Business)*.' I can understand the logic in this. Monkeys are intelligent animals and are quick to learn from human teachers, so the saying is well-based.

"Month of Sundays"

The Oxford English Dictionary states that the earliest printed usage of this phrase is:

> "1759, *H. Murray Life & Real Adventures*, Hamilton Murray I. x. 121 'The com-mander...swore he should dance to the second part of the tune, for a month of Sundays.'"

The Phrase Finder states "It seems very unlikely that this phrase was not a coinage by Mr. Murray, but rather something he was already familiar with because it was already in common use."

Of course the meaning is 'a very long while,' though this doesn't seem so long in today's way of thinking.

"My two cents worth"

There is a lack of agreement on the origin of this phrase, meaning a person's personal opinion, whether wanted or not.

The earliest reference to two small coins is in the *Bible* in both the Gospels of *Mark* and *Luke* in the story told by Jesus about the poor widow who had only two 'mites,' like our two cents today, to put in the Temple offering. Because this is all she has, Jesus states that it is of more value than the great sums given by those with so much more money. This would indicate that one person's two cents worth may be of more value than someone else's opinion. It is possible that this premise is the basis of the saying.

The American phrase, 'my two cents worth' is predated by the British one, 'two pence worth,' but is more widely used today.

Some believe that the idiom arose from a minimum ante into a poker game.

Others believe that it is derived from the much older sixteenth century English phrase, included in this volume, 'a penny for your thoughts,' 'two cents worth' possibly indicating more than asked for.

The first known printed reference to the American saying was in *The Olean Evening Times*, (New York) in March, 1926 and was written by Allene Sumner. The heading was: "My two cents' worth."

"My way or the highway"

Sir Thomas Eagleton (1540-1617), Lord Chancellor under Queen Elizabeth, wished to gain favor with the new monarch, King James I. To assure King James of his loyalty, he wrote:

> "I have learned no waye but the King's highway."

From this evolved our current cliché, 'My way or the highway.' The meaning is that 'if you don't like the way I want it done, you can hit the road.' It joins a lot of similar sayings, like 'Don't let the door hit your butt on the way out.'

N

"Ne'er do well"

This is a contraction of never do well, and originated in Scotland in the eighteenth century or before. A reference to it is found in Scottish poet and playwright Allan Ramsay's *A collection of Scots proverbs,* 1785.

> "Some ha'e a hontla faults, ye are only a ne'er do well."

The phrase refers to a worthless person; one in whom others have no hope for a fruitful future.

"Nip in the bud"

Living in the 'Nursery capitol of the world,' McMinnville, Tennessee, I ought to be a specialist in horticulture. I'm not. But that is the age-old origin of this term. In order to be more productive, trees and flowers have to be pruned. One item in proper pruning is nipping a number of less significant buds and allowing the healthy ones to receive a greater amount of the flower or tree's life-giving sap for nourishment.

The original phrase was 'nip in the bloom' and the earliest known reference to the phrase in a symbolic sense is in Henry Chettle's romance *Piers Plainnes Seaven Yeres Prentiship,* in 1595.

"Extinguish these fond loues with minds labour, and nip thy affections in the bloome, that they may neuer bee of power to budde."

Therefore, the idea of nipping undesirable notions 'in the bud' before they took the place of something more productive became a phrase to be commonly utilized.

"No spring chicken"

A precursor of this saying was recorded as early as 1711 by Richard Steele in *The Spectator.*

"You ought to consider you are now past a spring chicken..."

No spring chicken, as an idiom, was first recorded in 1906 in *The Encyclopedia of Word and Phrase Origins.*

One story is that in the early days of settling New England, chicken farmers discovered quickly that chickens born in the spring brought a better price that fall than older chickens which had gone through even one winter. Occasionally a farmer would try to pass off an older chicken for one born that spring. Upon examination, the buyers would remark, "That's no spring chicken!"

The phrase caught on and has long been used to apply to people, like so many of these old sayings. Once we have passed our youthful years, and we start to show the wear of life's 'ups and downs' (see), we realize that we are 'no spring chickens' any more.

"Not a dry eye in the house"

The etymology of this idiom is based on a special meaning of the word 'house' as everyone attending a performance in a theater or other meeting place. It is listed in *The Cambridge Dictionary of American Idioms*, because it was coined in the US. It means that the general mood of an audience is one of strong emotion to the point of tears.

The saying came into popular usage late in the twentieth century and inspired a rap song by that title, written by Duane Warren, and recorded by Meat Loaf, released in 1995.

"Not playing with a full deck"

In olden days, playing cards was popular entertainment. However, there was a tax levied on the purchase of cards, only applicable to the Ace of Spades. To avoid paying the tax, people would purchase only the other 51 cards. Yet, since most games require all 52 cards, these people were thought to be stupid because 'they weren't playing with a full deck.'

"Not worth a hill of beans"

This old adage is somewhat akin to 'don't know beans,' since beans have for centuries been classified as among the most worthless of the farm harvest. Remember the story of Jack and the beanstalk? But to me, this is a poor premise, as beans are good for so many things, and there are countless varieties of them. Soy beans, for example, have multiple uses and are among the most nutritious of crops.

The phrase 'a hill of beans' is of American origin, and refers to the beans from one dropping of beans in a row, usually two beans. It was used in a literal sense as early as 1858. It was used figuratively in the 1921 publication of *The Indiscretions of Archie,* a novel by P. G.

Wodehouse, published first in the UK, and immediately afterward in the US :

> "Here have I been kicking because you weren't a real burglar, when it doesn't amount to a hill of beans whether you are or not."

"Not worth your salt"

Millenniums ago, all or part of people's salary would be paid in salt. There is a mention of this in the Biblical book of *Ezra, chapter 6, verse 9,* in reference to the pay for the Persian king's servants. Also, according to the writings of Pliny the Elder in *Plinius Naturalias Historia XXXI,* the Roman soldiers were paid in salt. In fact, the Latin word 'salarium' is said to be the root of the English words salt, soldier, and salary.

"No walk in the park"

Let me tell you, it's 'no walk in the park' finding the origin of this idiom! It seems to have evolved in the twentieth century, and is more often used in the negative than the positive. A walk in the park is something like 'a piece of cake,' just a plain, simple task. But more likely you will hear someone bemoaning a difficult task as 'no walk in the park.' Evidently it comes from the fact that a walk in the park is a leisurely and enjoyable event.

O

"Off the cuff"

In olden days, dress shirt cuffs were made of celluloid. Writers on some occasions failed to have paper to take notes and writing them on the removable cuffs of their shirts became an accepted common practice. Later they would incorporate their notes into their journals or jot them down for use in their stories or novels. Hence, they were said to be 'off the cuff.' This has come to mean anything that is improvised.

"O.K."

I ordinarily would not include a saying consisting of only two letters, and I personally normally use the alternative spelling, 'okay.' But the reason I am putting this in is because of its uniquely unusual origins. And it's not as old as you may think.

The first printed example that has been found, to my knowledge, is from a 1790 court record in Sumner County, Tennessee, approximately

150 miles from where I now have called home for the major part of 33 years. The record was discovered in 1859 by a Tennessee historian named Albigence Waldo Putnam. In the records, Andrew Jackson said that he:

> "…proved a bill of sale from Hugh McGary to Gasper Mansker, for an uncalled good, which was O.K."

An early notation of our modern usage appears in 1815 on the hand-written diary of William Richardson, who had traveled from Boston to New Orleans about a month after the famous battle fought there by Jackson. In the note he stated, "We arrived ok." Here it is used to mean 'all well.'

It is believed that the actual derivation of the term was from a frequent misspelling of 'all correct' as 'ole korrect.'

The Boston Morning Post on 23 March 1839 carried an article using the term with the insinuation that this was indeed the origin. It ended this way:

> "…and his *train*-band, would have his 'contribution box,' et ceteras, *o.k.* — all correct — and cause the corks to fly, like *sparks*, upward."

One year later, when Martin Van Buren was running for his second term as President of the US the initials O.K. became a part of his campaign slogan. He was born in Kinderbrook, N.Y., and his nickname was Old Kinderbrook. His friends formed a committee for his campaign, called "The Democratic O.K. (Old Kinderbrook) Club." The slogan took off and he won the election.

Then on 23 October 1862, when James Pyle, placed an ad in *The New York Times,* referring to 'James Pyle's O.K. Soap' the term received even greater precedence, plunging it into everyday accepted English. Pyle's soap recipe was later purchased by Proctor and Gamble, and the name was changed to 'Ivory Snow.' Pyle's obituary in January, 1900, said that he was the first to use O.K. in an advertisement.

As a result of these varied events, O.K. came to mean something that was, well, you know, okay!

"Old battle ax"

A battle ax was used by the ancient Vikings as a weapon in battle. As they wore down, they would loosen on the handle and begin to rattle.

The phrase 'old battle ax' was coined from an American Women's Rights group in the nineteenth century to refer to a person who rattled on and on and didn't have much to say. I've met one or two of these in my day.

"Older than the hills"

I have heard this expression all my life and never knew that the root thought came from a verse in the *Bible, Job 15:7,* in a dialogue recorded as being between God and Job. God asks Job:

> "Are you the first man ever born, or were thou made before the hills?"

The first known example of the phrase in English, as we know it, is found in Francis Hutchinson's *A Defense of the Ancient Historians,* 1734.

> "As vales are as old as the hills, so loughs and rivers must be as old as they."

This seems likely to be a literal reference to hills. However, a figurative citation does come soon afterward in *The Edinburgh Magazine,* in Scotland, in 1787.

"If an unlucky gamester brought on his papyrus a combination of letters already known, every body abused him saying 'That has been already said' – 'That is as old as the hills' – 'all the world knows that.'"

"Old stomping grounds"

I know this one well. My 'old stomping grounds' is where I grew up and came of age. It's where I got my first whipping 'out behind the woodshed' and where I learned to pray and hoped God heard me before my dad got hold of me. For some it is a familiar spot to which they nostalgically like to return to have a good time.

This old pioneer-day saying came from the observations of settlers on the prancing of prairie chickens during their mating dances. They stomped and carried on so much that they wore out the ground, and soon the settlers could tell when an area had been their old stomping grounds.

It amazes me how many of the old sayings relating to animals, birds and the like turned up in metaphoric sayings about people. When only family is around—no company—in the South, we say, "There's nobody here but us chickens."

"Old warhorse"

This has come to mean a variety of things depending on who's talking. It can be an old standard well-loved play or piece of music which has lost its luster in the modern age; it may also apply to a retired person, often military, who was highly respected 'back in the day'(see), but has been 'put out to pasture'(see). Wow, we just keep thinking of other idioms, don't we now?

A warhorse was originally a vigilant charger employed by a gallant knight which dashed valiantly into battle. Later it was applied to a cavalryman. The phrase goes back to at least 1653. The following is from a journal published in June, 1887 titled *The Nation, Volume 44, Number 1146:*

> "The theatre of the war which broke out in **1653** between England and Holland, then at the height of her ... was the first land; to a son of the Anglo Saxon race, it was the old

home. ... He had bestridden the **war-horse** to good purpose ...″

During the American Civil War, in the 1860s, Confederate Commander, General Robert E. Lee greeted his close friend, General James Longstreet, calling him, 'my old war horse.' Afterward, 'War Horse' became Longstreet's nickname.

This likely plummeted the term into popular usage as we know it.

"Old wives' tale"

"Don't believe that nonsense, it's just an old wives' tale." In other words, something thought to have born from superstition and passed down by 'gossip.'

'Wife,' in this sense, meant any woman. This originated from the feeling that old people tend to live in the past, and what they say is to be 'taken with a grain of salt' (check this one out as well). *The King James Bible,* translated in 1611, uses a version of this. 'Refuse profane and old wives' fables' (*I Timothy 4:7*). But this saying was in use in England even before 1611—and strangely enough, this is the literal translation of the Greek—indicating that the thought had been around since at least the first century AD.

"On cloud nine"

One popular belief of the origin of this phrase has to do with cloud types. In the 1950s, the US Weather Bureau classified clouds using numbers for each type. Nine was the number of the fluffy cumulonimbus type which most people consider so beautiful as they float through the heavens. Someone on cloud nine would be enjoying a leisurely trip through the atmosphere.

Another explanation, and one of a much older origin, is that in Buddhism. Cloud Nine is one of the stages to Enlightenment of a Bodhisattva (one destined to become a Buddha).

The actual origin is in doubt, and earliest references are to other numbers for clouds, such as seven, eight and even thirty-one, and come from the mid twentieth century in the US. One such is first listed in Albin Pollock's directory of slang, *The Underworld Speaks*, published in 1935.

"Cloud eight, befuddled on account of drinking too much liquor."

Perhaps this was saying that the person fell a bit short of cloud nine?

Actual printed references to 'cloud nine' come a bit later. In August 1946, the magical month of my appearance on planet earth, in the *Oxnard Press Currier* in California.

"I think he thought of everything, unless the authorities put something new on him out of cloud nine."

The early favorite, however, was cloud seven. In *The Dictionary of American Slang*, originally published in 1960, we find:

"Cloud seven – completely happy, perfectly satisfied, in a euphoric state."

According to the Internet site, *The Phrase Finder*, to which I owe a lot of this information, this may have been influenced by the popular saying, 'in seventh heaven.'

"One bad apple spoils the whole barrel"

Well, now here's a difficult saying to trace. I've also heard it said as 'spoils the whole bunch,' or 'bushel' as well. But the origin of the thought was something a bit different entirely. It seems to have been a Chinese proverb. The oldest version was 'One mouse dropping ruins the whole pot of rice.' Yuck! But the core idea remains the same: one person's bad or negative example can rub off on many more.

It is a bit uncertain exactly when this was converted to the English version with apples. It likely is a variant from the quotation from a fourteenth century Latin proverb translated, 'The rotten apple injures its neighbors.'

It may be that it first appeared in English when Geoffrey Chaucer used the idea in his unfinished work, *The Cook's Tale:*

> "Better take a rotten apple from the hoard /
> Than let it lie to spoil the good ones there."

These proverbs carry the meaning that the solution is ridding the barrel of the bad apple.

"One red cent"

How many times have you heard someone say that something is not worth 'one red cent?' Some have supposed that this came from the original Native American, called at that time a 'red man,' on the front of the 'Indian head penny.' Not so.

This term is derived from the red color or the pure copper that 'pennies' or cent coins in America were originally made from. Now they are more of a brown color, because they are made from an alloy of copper, tin and zinc. And of course, they are not nearly worth one red cent.

"Out of the frying pan and into the fire"

This idea goes back to many ancient civilizations. In second century Greece, it was 'Out of the smoke and into the flame.' In Italian, as well as Portuguese, it was roughly, 'Out of the frying pan and into the coals,' The Gaelic equivalent is 'Out of the cauldron and into the fire.' The French version is more like today's English one. It would be translated, 'To leap from the frying pan into the fire,' and may be the immediate forerunner of our phrase.

This cliché means that a situation is bad and about to get worse.

"Out of the woods"

This commonly-used expression, now referring to being out of imminent danger, particularly of death or financial ruin, had its origin in Roman times, when it had to do with an actual forest.

Its first known written usage in England was in the eleventh century by Charles Kingsley in *Hereward the Wake.* The British version is 'out of the wood.'

As a *proverb*, however, it originated in the United States, and was referenced in the papers of Benjamin Franklin. It was used by Abigail Adams in a letter dated 13 November 1800.

"Out the ying yang"

Though etymologists find it difficult to pin down the origin of the phrases 'out the ying yang,' meaning having an abundance of something and 'up the ying yang,' the meaning of which seems a bit obscure, I find it difficult to believe it had nothing to do with the Chinese symbol, yin yang, which I have posted below.

 This ancient philosophical symbol represents a balance in humans and in all of nature between light and dark, and good and evil. It is a Tao symbol which has been around since the Yellow Empire (2698BC to 2598BC). The possession of this balance represents an abundance of peace in one's life.

An Atlanta-based American crunk rap duo debuting in 2000 took the name "The Ying Yang Twins," and has enjoyed popularity in the hip-hop community.

The term ying yang is likely a corruption of yin yang, and could have been coined by young people who were bothered by comparisons of the 'great wisdom' of the ancient cultures, and meant it as a sign of being fed up. This is often used in the connotation of "I've had it up the ying yang with this," which may have been enlarged to mean anything in abundance. Just my 'two cents worth' (see).

"Over a barrel"

This saying, which has been around since at least 1938, is American in origin, and means under someone else's emotional or financial control and unable to do anything about it.

The first known reference to the phrase is in a cartoon in *The Clearfield Progress*, a newspaper published in Pennsylvania. I have included the cartoon below (see cliché, bottom right).

OUR BOARDING HOUSE, with MAJOR HOOPLE

From the caption of this cartoon, it appears that the phrase was in use prior to the publication.

On the Origin of the Clichés & Evolution of Idioms

There seems to be some confusion as to
whether this meant a wooden barrel, which
may be smothering someone, or a gun barrel,
as seemed to be the case in a later reference.

P

"Paddle your own canoe"

This means to take charge of your own life, and is, I would say, for the most part, good advice. It has been in use since the early nineteenth century. At least two poems in the mid 1800s went by this title. The following is one of them, is anonymous, and was published in 1852 in the *Crawford County Courier* in Wisconsin.

Paddle Your Own Canoe

My father die, God rest his soul,
When years I numbered two,
And left me 'midst this world alone,
To paddle my own canoe.

A step-grand-daddy, now no more,
Taught me my P's and Q.
And ever in my ears he dinned,
You'll paddle your own canoe.

My home was no Elysian spot
Of bright and sunny hue,
And therefore I the sooner left,
To paddle my own canoe.

On the Origin of the Clichés & Evolution of Idioms

And through the world I roamed at large,
O'er land and ocean blue;
And though the struggle oft was hard,
I paddled my own canoe.

For thus I argued, man to man,
Is often, times untrue;
Then while with health and strength you're
blest
Just paddle your own canoe.

As partners in the strife for gain,
Self-interest will pursue;
And leave you with your debts, perhaps,
To paddle your own canoe.

And then no sympathy you'll find
From friends who once were true;
They knew you lost when first you ceased
To paddle your own canoe.

But I one cherished object sought
And ever kept in view;
A friend of pure unsullied heart,
'To paddle my own canoe.

A friend she is in word and deed —
Her interest mine is too;
The twain are one - I still may say,
I paddle my own canoe.

"Paint the town red"

My, oh my! Excitement and having a good time, regardless of the consequences, are associated with 'painting the town red.'

The most likely place of origin for this phrase is in Melton Mowbray, Leicestershire, in the UK, based on a well-documented event which took place in 1837. That year, Henry de la Poer Beresford, the Marquis of Waterford, a 'notorious hooligan,' took a group of his friends and 'ran riot' throughout the town, painting the toll-bar and several buildings red.

Painting, *New Sporting Magazine,* **July 1837**

"Passing the buck"

Passing responsibility on to someone else rather than doing the job yourself is called 'passing the buck.' It is a phrase that comes from card games where bucks are used to indicate the dealer (see: **buck stops here, The**).

"Peeping Tom"

According to a well-known legend, a man named Leofric taxed the people of Coventry, England excessively. His wife, the famous Lady Godiva, begged him to let up on the taxation. Leofric said he would end the tax if she rode through the streets of the city naked; so she agreed, and did so.

Peeping Tom is a much later addition to this story. Everybody in Coventry was told to stay indoors with the shutters closed. However, it is told that one man, later dubbed 'Peeping Tom,' sneaked a look at Godiva and was struck blind.

The term came to mean any man who looked in on women who were indisposed without their knowledge.

"penny for your thoughts, A"

A penny hardly seems a fair price to obtain a person's innermost meditations in the twenty-first century. This statement, however, originated in a time when a penny was something more to be sought after — even earlier than the time of the next proverb.

It was mentioned in 1522 by Sir Thomas More in *Four Last Things*.

Playwright John Heywood included 'A penny for your thoughts' in his catalogue of proverbs in 1546, in which the reference to 'A byrde in the hande' was made.

The saying likely dates further back, as the penny has a long history in Britain. The silver penny was first made about 757 AD, and by the reign of King Edward III in the fourteenth century, it was the most important coin in circulation, worth 1/12 of a shilling.

The *Straight Dope* web site calculated a sixteenth century English penny to have been worth the equivalent of $42.67 in 2001 value. However, in purchasing power, it seems from other sources that was not the case, but more like two to four dollars. Still, in John Heywood's day, a penny for one's thoughts may have been something to consider.

"penny saved is a penny earned, A"

The credit for this bit of wisdom goes to Benjamin Franklin, and appeared in his publication *Poor Richard's Almanac* in the eighteenth century. Today it would likely be 'a dollar saved,' at the very least. The point of the proverb is to encourage guarding against waste, and spending that which may be laid back 'for a rainy day.'

"People who live in glass houses shouldn't throw stones"

No one will argue the meaning of this phrase. Those who have faults should not strike out at others. It's like 'the pot calling the kettle black.'

This proverb goes back to Geoffrey Chaucer's *Troilus and Criseyde* in 1385.

Then, George Herbert wrote in 1651:

"Whose house is of glass, must not throw stones at another."

This saying is first cited in the US in 1710 in *William & Mary College Quarterly.*

Twenty-six years later Benjamin Franklin wrote in *Poor Richard's Almanac:*

"Don't throw stones at your neighbors', if your own windows are glass."

Random House Dictionary of Popular Proverbs and Sayings, 1996, says, "'To live in a glass house' is used as a figure of speech referring to vulnerability."

"Piece of cake"

The idea for this phrase originated in the southern United States way back in 1870s, when cakes were given out as prizes for winning competitions. Slave couples used to walk in a circle around a cake at a gathering. The most graceful pair would win the cake. This is also the origin of 'cake walk,' both meaning that something was easy to accomplish.

On the Origin of the Clichés & Evolution of Idioms

The first written usage of the cliché was in *Primrose Path*, in 1936, by the outstanding American poet, Ogden Nash.

> "Her picture's in the papers now,
> and life's a piece of cake."

"Pie in the sky"

Pie in the sky, often suffixed with 'by and by,' or the original, 'when you die.'

"Pie in the sky" comes from an early twentieth century folk song titled *The Preacher and the Slave* written by labor activist Joe Hill, aka Joe Hillstrom, born Joel Emmanuel Hillgglund, a legendary member of the labor group, Industrial Workers of the World. The song, a parody of the hymn *In the Sweet By and By*, was written in 1911 and is a satire on the Salvation Army, the preachers of whom Hill decried for lulling workers into complacency. The phrase is in the first verse.

> "You will eat, bye and bye,
> In that glorious land above the sky;
> Work and pray, live on hay
> You'll get pie in the sky when you die."

Hill was executed for a murder of which he was likely not guilty in 1915. While the song sank into oblivion, lost in the annals of forgotten history, the saying caught on 'like wildfire' and came to mean any empty promises which would never be fulfilled. Flowery political speeches prior to elections were often placed into the category.

Joe Hill

"Pitch black"

Pitch is a substance originally made from tree sap, now also derived from coal tar or petroleum. It appears like tar, and was anciently used as waterproofing. It is mentioned in the *Bible* as the agent applied to Noah's ark to make it shed the water of the great flood. Since it is undeniably dark, the original saying was 'black as pitch.' Over the years it became simply, 'pitch black.' Sometimes this is used to describe a night at its darkest hour, when the heavenly bodies are obscured by dense clouds. Also, this could be utilized as a metaphor of a person's worst life experiences. In Latin it was pic, and in Old English it was pich.

The phrase has been around for a long time, and its exact origin is somewhat obscure.

"Play 'possum"

I've heard this one all my life, because I was brought up in the country and know what it means. When an opossum is under attack by a predator, they have an internal defense mechanism, much like that of the skunk which causes it to secrete its lovely perfume, but the opossum's is non-threatening. It simply curls up and pretends to be dead, and then the attacker goes away. I've seen this spectacle a number of times in my youth.

As to when and where it came into use as an idiom, I can't seem to find anyone who knows. But it has likely been around for centuries among those who have the opportunity to greet 'possums on occasion. When, like many of these other animal personifications, it applies to a person, it means that they pretend to be either dead or in most cases, only asleep, to avoid a confrontation with someone with whom they don't care to associate, or don't want to talk with at that precise moment.

"Poetic justice"

The British literary critic and historian, Thomas Rymer, coined the phrase 'poetic justice' in his essay, *The Tragedies of the Last Age Considere'd* in 1678. It means the allocation of an ideal form of justice, where virtue is rewarded and infamy punished, as befitting a poetry of drama.

"Poor as a church mouse"

This phrase, meaning 'impoverished,' originated, and was very popular, in the seventeenth century. It seems that there was a tale told of a mouse which took refuge in a church, and looked everywhere for food. Since churches of that era had no kitchens, the poor mouse was destined to go hungry.

The following quote is from *Political Ballads*, 1731:

> "The owner, 'tis said, was once poor as a churchmouse."

"Poor as Job's turkey"

The word 'poor' has been around since 1200 AD, and old Job, well, he's been around for longer than 'a coon's age.' This expression is credited to a Canadian judge and humorist named Thomas Haliburton (1796-1865), using the pseudonym Sam Slick, and appeared in the mid nineteenth century. He described Job's turkey as so poor he had only one brother, and so weak he had to lean against a fence in order to gobble.

The book of *Job* in the *Bible* is believed to be the oldest of biblical writings, even before there was such a thing as an Israelite. It is the tale of a wealthy man who was taunted by the devil with the permission of God. After he had everything taken away and was lying in ashes with boils all over him, he still had faith in the Supreme Being. He was used as an example of patience. To be 'poor as Job's turkey' indicated the lowest estate imaginable. Job, of course, would not have had a turkey, as they are native to North America.

"Potluck"

This term actually had its origin in the Middle Ages in Europe. The *original* potluck was a celebration. The host would give away his possessions.

The tradition of potluck comes from the frugal idea of never throwing anything away. In days of old meal leftovers were thrown into a pot together to feed unexpected guests. If you were to share a meal with a family you often had to take 'the luck of the pot,' as you could never be quite sure what you would be served.

"Pound of flesh"

Many, like I did, will immediately recognize this phrase as being from Shakespeare's *Merchant of Venice*.

"SHYLOCK:
The pound of flesh which I demand of him
Is deerely bought, 'tis mine, and I will haue
it."

The insistence of Shylock that Antonio pay with his very flesh is central to the plot of the play.

Though *Merchant of Venice* debuted in 1586, the idiom did not become a part of our culture until the late eighteenth century. It is used to refer to a lawful but unreasonable payment of anything thought to be owed, and likely long overdue.

"Pushing the envelope"

Now used to mean carrying anything beyond the reasonable point, this idiom had its beginnings in the 1940s United States Air Force test pilot program. It originally meant flying an aircraft beyond its known performance 'envelope' or recommended limits.

"Pushing up daisies"

Daisies and other flowers of the field have long figured in the botanical image of dying and being buried. Flowers are sometimes planted on graves. Daisies seem to be most common. In *The Babes in the Woods,* a narrative poem about the Norfolk tragedy, included in *The Ingoldsby Legends,* Rev. Richard Barham (written in the early nineteenth century) tells us to:

> "...be kind to those wee little folks
> When our toes are turned up to the daisies."

In 1866 George Macdonald polished this cute phrase by saying:

> "I shall very soon hide my name under some daisies."

Today, in America, we use 'pushing up daisies' to mean when we are no longer among those running through the meadows looking down upon them, and our mortal shell lies below the soil.

"Put out to pasture"

The word pasture is form the Middle English, and derived from the Latin *pastura*, meaning 'grazing.' Cows or horses which are thought to be past the age to bare young and, in the case of cattle, give milk are put out to pasture, and sometimes sold for various purposes…food for carnivorous animals, dog food, etc.

The term 'put out to pasture' gradually came to apply to humans who were past their productive years, and means 'forced to retire.' It is equally popular in both England and the US. I have not been able to pin down a first date of printed reference.

"Put that in your pipe and smoke it"

Mickey Mouse has another version of this famous cliché—'Put that in your smoke and pipe it!' The first known citation was made by R. B. Peake in his two-act comedy, *American Abroad*, in 1824. It was exactly as we know it.

Then, in *The Lay of St. Odille,* 1856 by the same author as *The Babes in the Woods*, mentioned above, Rev. Richard H. Barham:

"Put that in your pipe, my lord Otto, and smoke it!"

There are other more recent quotations, but you get the picture. It means 'digest that!' 'Think about what I have said very carefully.'

"Putting all the cards on the table"

The origin of this phrase, unsurprisingly, is from card games in which placing all of one's cards open is an act of honesty and truthfulness. Not something done very often in poker or blackjack!

Though I have not been able to find the actual first usage, the saying has been around a long time, just as card games have.

Putting all of one's cards on the table means to be completely honest about one's purpose and intentions.

"Put up your dukes"

Well, we all know this challenge to fistfight someone. It goes back to Prince Frederick Augustus, the Duke of York and Albany at the time of King George III of England in the late eighteenth and early nineteenth centuries. Prince Frederick, it was said, loved to duel, so fighters nicknamed their fists 'Dukes of York.' This was eventually shortened to simply 'dukes.'

"Put your best foot forward"

I would never have realized that this was such an old expression. *The Random House Dictionary of Popular Proverbs and Sayings* dates the origin of this back to 1495, but offers no documentation.

The first known printed reference to a similar phrase is from a poem titled *A Wife* by Thomas Overbury in 1613.

"Hee is still setting the best foot forward."

This, of course, applied to the *right* foot (see 'getting up on the wrong side of the bed'). Your best foot is actually an incorrect adage, and should have been coined as 'better foot,' since it implies a person has more than two feet. Shakespeare, who has given us a number of our popular idioms, used a form of this one in *King John*.

"Nay, but make haste; the better foot before."

This means that a person should embark on a task with singleness of purpose and determination to succeed.

Q

"Quick and the dead"

This is a biblical reference to the living and the dead, and is found in the *Bible* in several places, all referring to the final judgment of man. The first time it appeared in English was in the *Wycliffe Bible* in 1385 (*II Timothy 4:1*). Later it appeared in the *King James Version* in 1611. The phrase *The Quick and the Dead* became the title of a movie released in 1995 staring Sharon Stone. Here it referred to being either literally quick or dead in a Western town containing gunfighters.

"Quick as a wink"

This saying was first recorded in 1825 in *Words and Phrase Origins* by Robert Hendrickson. A more modern variant is 'quick as a flash.' Another such phrase is 'in the twinkling of an eye,' taken from the *Bible (I Corinthians 15:52)*.

"Quick as greased lightening"

The British expression from which it derived was 'quick as lightening.' Thomas Comber used this simile in 1676 in his devotional, *A Companion to the Temple:*

> "Now if the Attendants be bright as the Sun, quick as Lightning, and powerful as Thunder; what is He that is their Lord?"

Lightening, of course, has for many centuries been a symbol of speed, and using greased just intensifies the meaning. The first known references to greased lightening are from the early nineteenth century. The British newspaper, *The Boston, Lincoln. Louth & Spalding Herald* ran a story in January 1833 including these words:

> "He spoke as quick as 'greased lightening.'"

"Quid pro quo"

Though not exactly a cliché, and not really English, either, it is certainly a phrase to know, not only the meaning, but the origin. Indicating doing a deed in return for something the other does for you, 'You scratch my back, I'll scratch yours' comes to mind (see), it is Latin, and dates to the day when Shakespeare used a version of it in *Henry VI* in 1591.

"I cry you mercy, 'tis but Quid for Quo."

"Quiet as a mouse"

This term dates back to the 1500s. Who can imagine any creature more still than a little mouse in search for food in the middle of the night. It wouldn't even awaken the lightest sleeper.

"Quit your bellyaching"

Haven't found out how long this has been around, but it's a popular saying in America. It means 'stop whining and complaining.' It may have evolved from 'quit telling me about your belly ache.'

R

"Raining cats and dogs"

There are a number of theories as to this phrase, but it's been in use for 'a coon's age' (see). One belief is that thunder and lightening represent a dog and cat fight. I just don't buy that one very much.

Some say that in London in the time of the bubonic plague during hard rains bodies of infected cats and dogs would wash up in the gutters. Perhaps.

But this phrase was around back in the dark ages according to historians. Cats were believed by superstitious sailors to have a lot to do with producing storms. And remember the witches who were said to ride the storms were often pictured on black cats.

Dogs and wolves were symbols of winds, and the Norse storm god, Odin, was frequently shown with dogs and wolves hovered around him. In the saying, 'raining cats and dogs,' cats symbolize the rain, and dogs the wind. So now, I've 'let the cat out of the bag' (see) on this one.

"Read between the lines"

The story is told that this phrase came from the early days of sending secret messages. Messages would be written on regular paper but hidden to be revealed only when a substance called a 're-agent' was applied.

Since delivering a blank sheet of paper was a dead giveaway, letters would be delivered by currier containing a message of little or no importance, but to read the true message, the recipient would have to apply the re-agent to the spaces between the lines, where the true message would then appear, perhaps when held up to light.

Another way of achieving this in the early nineteenth century was to write something where the recipient could read in the true meaning based on knowledge which they had and others did not. This was a simple form of cryptography of the day.

An early example of this phrase in text was found printed in the *New York Times* in August 1862.

"Earl Russell's dispatch does not recite the terms of the note to which it is a reply, the letter assumes a somewhat enigmatical character, and the only resource we have is, as best we may, to 'read between the lines' of this puzzling, but important, communication of the British Foreign Secretary."

"Read the Riot Act"

Nobody looks forward to being read the riot act by a family member or someone in authority over them. Today it is used in jest and means to be scolded or told off for something they have done.

But the real Riot Act was no joke. Following this law, enacted by the government in Britian in July 1715 (The full title was *An act for preventing tumults and riotous assemblies, and for the more speedy and effectual punishing the rioters*), if a rowdy group of twelve or more people gathered, a magistrate would read an official statement ordering them to disperse at once. It was enacted in haste to prevent Catholic Jacobite rebels from protesting against George I. Anyone who did not comply, after one hour, could be arrested and punished. The Jacobites supported the Scottish House of Stewart, and were a real threat to the new Hanoverian king.

"Red letter day"

All of us have seen Sundays on a calendar in red numbers, and other days in black. The practice began in ancient times when monks made, and were the only ones who kept calendars. They were made by hand in monasteries or convents. Scribes often emphasized Saints Days, or festival days by marking them with a reddish ink made with ocher, a mineral of oxide of iron.

Later, when calendars began to be printed for common use, those in Christian countries often made the numbers of Sunday in red. This pattern caused the adaption of the idiom 'red letter day' for an important day in someone's life, like their wedding day, birthday, or graduation from college.

The first specific reference to this term comes from America, from the diary of Sarah Knight in *The Journals of Madam Knight and the Reverend Mister Buckingham*, written in 1704 and 1710, and published in 1940 in *American Speech*.

"Resting on your laurels"

In the ancient world, winners in athletics and other heroes were distinguished by awarding them wreaths of laurel leaves. If they rested on their laurels it meant that they were relying on their past achievements, and not reaching out for new goals. It still means this today.

"Rings true"

Contrary to some folks' belief, this saying came into being, not from the toll of a bell, but from the quality if a coin.

During the Middle Ages, due to the scarcity of precious metals, and the scarcity of equipment, metalworkers were not able to produce coins that were uniform in size and appearance. I have some ancient coins which certainly bear this out. Because of this, criminals took advantage of the situation, and counterfeit coins were common. When there was any doubt as to a coin's authenticity, a merchant would drop it on a stone slab to observe its sound. If the coin was phony, it would make a dull tone. A true coin would make a clear sound, or ring. Thus the saying 'ring true' was born. The other hollow sound was called 'ringing false.'

Today if something sounds like a true statement based on known facts, it is said to 'ring true.'

"rolling stone gathers no moss, A"

This sixteenth century proverb is based on a principle well-known in that era. Moss is a very slow-growing organism. The easiest way to keep it from forming on rocks is to move them about on a regular basis. The first known printing of it is by our old friend and publisher of curious English phrases, John Heywood, in 1546, in *A dialogue conteinyng the number in effect of all the prouerbes in the Englishe tongue*. It means that unless one settles down, they will never really accomplish anything.

"The rollyng stone neuer gatherth mosse."

Even before this a form of it was included by Erasmus in the third volume of his Latin proverbs, *Adagia*, in 1508.

"Rome wasn't built in a day"

This well-worn proverb is another for which sixteenth century British playwright and writer John Heywood, mentioned above, must also receive credit for passing it on to us. It was also in *A dialogue conteinying the number in effect of all the prouerbes in the Englishe tongue,* published in 1546.

It means that nothing good happens overnight. It takes time to build relationships, businesses, etc.

"Rub the wrong way"

Nobody wants to be rubbed the wrong way, and everyone knows what it means. But this term was originally something else entirely. In colonial America, floors of the better homes were made of wide oak boards which were polished by the servants once a week so that when company came they would look their best. It was imperative that this be done by rubbing with the grain, because 'rubbing the wrong way' would cause unsightly streaking.

S

"Sadder but wiser"

Since the definition of the word cliché from dictionary.com included this one, I felt a bit obligated to include it. Sadder but wiser came into its own as a result of the 1962 version of *Music Man*, starring Robert Preston. The title to a song in this popular Rogers and Hammerstein musical extravaganza was *The Sadder-But-Wiser Girl for Me*. The song ended like this:

> "Why, she's the fisherman, I'm the fish you see? — PLOP!
> I flinch, I shy, when the lass with the delicate air goes by
> I smile, I grin, when the gal with a touch of sin walks in.
> I hope, and I pray, for a Hester to win just one more 'A'
> The sadder-but-wiser girl's the girl for me.
> The sadder-but-wiser girl for me."

The term has come to mean that as a result of an unpleasant event or circumstance, a person has become more aware and acceptant.

"Saved by the bell"

The most logical explanation for this saying is the boxer who is being beaten to a pulp and the bell announces the end of the round. This came into use as a boxing term in the late nineteenth century, but its origins go back to as early as the seventeenth century.

The term, however, originally applied to being saved by a ringing bell attached to a coffin to keep people from being buried alive due to a lack of medical understanding and unconsciousness. People were often pronounced dead when they were in comas, seizures, and other states of near-death. There were several patients in England and early America who opted for 'safety coffins' with bells incorporated into the designs which would ring in the event of body movement. These special coffins were registered in the late 1800s and as late as 1955. This is also where the saying 'dead ringer' (see) originated.

"Save it for a rainy day"

It may surprise you to know that this saying has been around in English, according to *The Dictionary of Clichés* by James Rogers, since

1580, when it was used by Francis Kinwelmersh in his frightening tale, *The Bugbears.*

> "'Wold he haue me kepe nothing against a raynye day?'"

This joins such favorites as 'A penny saved is a penny earned,' and brings to mind the old Perry Como lyric, 'Catch a falling star and put it in your pocket, save it for a rainy day.'

"Say uncle!"

Many believe that this expression came from the old Irish word 'anacol,' meaning the act of deliverance, protection, or mercy, as it is used to beg for mercy when someone has carried a friendly induction of pain a wee bit too far.

Another theory is that it goes even further back to a Latin expression used by Roman youth who got into trouble, *patrue mi patruissime,* meaning uncle, my best of uncles. They are thought to have been required to call for their uncle in order to be freed.

A number of newspapers in the late nineteenth and early twentieth centuries carried jokes with reference to this practice, often in the children's section.

One such example is from the *Iowa Citizen,* October 9, 1891:

> *A gentleman was boasting that his parrot would repeat anything he told him. For example, he told him several times, before some friends, to say "Uncle," but the parrot would not repeat it. In anger he seized the bird, and half-twisting his neck, said: "Say 'uncle,' you beggar!" and threw him into the fowl pen, in which he had ten prize fowls. Shortly afterward, thinking he had killed the parrot, he went to the pen. To his surprise he found nine of the fowls dead on the floor with their necks wrung, and the parrot standing on the tenth twisting his neck and screaming: "Say 'uncle,' you beggar! say uncle.'"*

"Scot free"

I know what you're probably thinking. This is a slam against the Scottish people, possibly something to do with penny-pinching. Nope, it's actually form the Old English word *sceot,* which meant a tax or a penalty. People in England who avoided taxes in olden days were said to have gotten off 'scot free.' Do you reckon there are any folks doing this today?

"Second fiddle"

This has a similar meaning to 'taking a back seat' to someone or something else, or be subordinate to them. Some people equate it to a 'sidekick' of an important person, and it evolved in the same time frame (see that entry below).

In an orchestra, the second 'fiddle,' or violin, plays more of a harmony than that played by the more prominent lead violin. Therefore the second fiddle is somewhat overpowered by the lead, though it still plays an important part to the value of the music.

"Sell yourself short"

Novices are often admonished by their leaders not to sell themselves short in a business deal, or not to lack confidence in their own abilities to perform a task when they have the capability to do so.

This expression came from selling stock. Selling a stock short actually means to sell stock you don't own. These shares can be bought later before the transaction is completed. This is practiced when investors believe the price of stock is going down and they hope to profit in that drop. This is one reason that insider trading is forbidden.

Selling stock short is an anticipation of decline in price, thus selling yourself short came to mean that you are or feel that you are loosing ability in some area.

"Shaking like a leaf"

This is another of many metaphoric expressions likely originating in the latter half of the twentieth century in America. It is used most commonly by someone who is terrified of a given situation into which they are thrust. It indicates that they are trembling with anxiety, like a leaf on a tree blowing in the wind.

"Shoo-in"

Some misspell this as shoe-in. It has come to mean a sure winner, but was not started this way. Originally, the verb shoo meant to take someone or something in a specific direction by making noises or gestures.

The shift of this expression to horse racing occurred some time in the early twentieth century. It meant winning a rigged race. George E. Smith related how this came about in his highly-acclaimed, *Racing Maxims and Methods of Pittsburgh Phil* in 1908.

> "There were many times presumably that 'Tod' would win through such manipulations, being 'shooed in,' as it were".

 **George E. Smith, 1903**

"Shoot fire and save matches"

Well, I can't tell you exactly when this saying started or who coined it, but I can say that everyone I know says it started in the American South at least by the mid twentieth century. When I was growing up "in the sticks" we used it as an expression of surprise, alarm or disgust. If something didn't go the way we felt it should, we'd dang it and say "shoot fire and save matches." I have heard folks use a little more colorful version.

"Show your true colors"

Early warships often carried flags of many nations aboard, in order to deceive the enemy and possibly ward off an attack, or get the jump on the enemy before they realized who they were. However, the rules of warfare required the ship to hoist the country's true colors before firing on another ship. It has come to mean showing forth one's true personality or intent, especially when it is not what the other expected.

"Sidekick"

We who grew up watching black and white TV Westerns on Saturday mornings were first introduced to the term sidekick by such heroes as Roy Rogers with Pat Brady, the Cisco Kid and Pancho, and the Lone Ranger and Tonto. However, the actual origin of this term was much less benign. It was originally a close confidant in crime, first appearing in underworld slang in 1906.

How it came to first be coined is in question. To a pickpocket, a kick is a pair of trousers, and most specifically denoted as being trouser pockets. 'Kick' (a word used to mean pockets) first appeared in the mid nineteenth century, and even today 'kick' is used for a roll of bills or a stash of money. The term sidekick could have developed as someone who was kept up by a thief who divided up the spoils and provided a home for those who would come up beside a victim and snatch the 'kick.' It came to mean a person who was kicked to the side.

"Sitting duck"

As any duck hunter knows, a duck or goose sitting on a pond is much easier to hit than one in flight. It's sorta like taking candy from a baby, huh? Therefore, by the early twentieth century a 'sitting duck' became synonymous with anyone who was an easy mark, to harm or to scam.

"Sixteen Penny Nails"

There have been various reasons given for why nails are sized in "pennies" rather than length. Here is the correct one.

The word 'penny,' in this case, was an old English term used to describe the number of *pennies* required to purchase one hundred nails. Today the term is used only as a measurement of the length of the nail. A common sixteen-penny nail used in general construction today has a standard length of 3.5 inches, a number eight gauge diameter shaft (0.162 inches), a head diameter of $11/32^{nds}$ of an inch and forty-four such nails will weigh one pound.

"$64,000 question"

I had heard this all my life, and never known its origin. It had its roots in the CBS radio quiz show, *Take It or Leave It*, which ran from April 21, 1940, to July 27, 1947. The show was first hosted by Bob Hawk, who passed it to Phil Baker in '41. In 1947, the series switched to NBC, with various hosts including Baker, Garry Moore, Eddie Cantor and Jack Paar. On September 10, 1950, *Take It or Leave It* changed its title to *The $64 Question*. Paar continued as host, and then was followed by Baker from March to December of 1951, when Paar returned. The series continued on NBC Radio until June 1, 1952.

On both shows, contestants were asked questions written by researcher Edith Oliver. After answering correctly, the contestant was asked to either take or leave the prize money offered, or move on to a more difficult question which offered double the money. The first was worth $1 USD, and the final was the '$64.00 question.'

During the 1940s, 'That's the $64.00 question' became a common catch-phrase meaning the answer a difficult situation.

From 1955 to 1958, a version of the show aired on television under the title, *The $64,000 Question.* A spin-off show called *The $64,000 Challenge* was on between 1956 and 1958.

Nowadays the inflationary phrase is 'That's the $64,000,000 question.' What will it be in another sixty-four years?

"Skeleton in the closet"

This was originally coined in England, but since the British use the word 'closet' to mean a water closet, or commode, there it is now used as 'skeleton in the cupboard.'

The meaning of the phrase is 'a deep secret, that is being hidden, which, if exposed might cause irrefutable harm.' The first reference to this idiom is in the early nineteenth century. It is in an article by William Hendry Stowell in the UK monthly periodical *The Electric Review* in 1816. It is figurative in nature and the 'skeleton' was the supposed need to keep a hereditary disease secret.

"Two great sources of distress are the danger of contagion and the apprehension of hereditary diseases. The dread of being the cause of misery to posterity has prevailed over men to conceal the skeleton in the closet..."

The dramatic use of hidden bodies was found quite frequently in the Gothic novels and short stories of the Victorian age. Edgar Allan Poe, whose immortal works grace a shelf of my library, was a master of such tales. Here is an example from *The Black Cat*, first published in the *Saturday Evening Post* 1843:

"'Gentlemen, I delight to have allayed your suspicions,' and here, through the mere frenzy of bravado, I rapped heavily upon that very portion of the brick-work behind which stood the corpse of the wife of my bosom. The wall fell bodily. The corpse, already greatly decayed, stood erect before the eyes of the spectators."

Some feel that this phrase is derived from the era of the body snatchers, prior to 1832, when England allowed more extensive medical research of corpses due to the Anatomy Act.

Popular Victorian author William Makepeace Thackeray referred explicitly to 'skeletons in closets' in *The Newcomes; memoirs of a most respectable family*, 1857:

"Some particulars regarding the Newcome family, which will show us that they have a skeleton or two in their closets, as well as their neighbours."

"Slim Pickings"

This cliché originated in the early seventeenth century, and alluded to the remainder of a carcass which had been picked clean by wild animals.

It has come to symbolize the meager amount of food, clothing, etc. after the bulk has been plundered through. It is applied to the poorest of persons and their desperate attempts to survive in a 'dog-eat-dog' (see) world.

The expression inspired American rodeo performer turned comedy character actor, Louis Burton Lindley, Jr. (1919-1983), to take the stage name 'Slim Pickins.' Pickens 'epitomized the tough, profane, sardonic cowboy' in such films as *Dr. Strangelove* and *Blazing Saddles*.

"Snake in the grass"

The imagery of this metaphoric cliché goes back to many ancient sources and folklore. The earliest is likely the biblical book of *Genesis*, or beginnings. In *Genesis 3*, the story is told of how the serpent, or snake, used as a type of the devil, through subtlety, slithered its way into Eve's intellect and convinced her to take a bite of the 'forbidden fruit.'

The origin of the word 'snake' began in the Indo-European root word meaning 'to creep.' This meaning crept down to the Old High German word 'snahhan,' (to crawl), then the Old Norse 'snakr,' and the Old English word, 'snaca.' You get the picture. By Middle English it was already snake.

An ancient Chinese proverb states, "He who is bitten by the snake avoids tall grass."

The snake's craftiness and subtlety coupled with its slithering through the grass to attack its prey has been long used in both literal and figurative senses.

A 'snake in the grass' has come to be an unmistakable image of an untrustworthy, deceitful person.

"Snake oil"

True snake oil originated in China, and is from the Chinese Water Snake. It was used as a cure for rheumatoid arthritis and joint pain. Snake oil also played a role in ancient Egyptian medicine, and was blended with the fats of other animals such as lions, hippopotamuses, crocodiles, etc. It was believed by the masses that it could grow hair on bald men.

Chinese laborers working in America on the trans-continental railroad lines introduced snake oil to Europeans to cure joint pain. There were no regulations in North America in the nineteenth century regarding drugs, so when charlatans got hold of it, all sorts of fake oils were created. These were hawked by the traveling salesmen who went about the country with their medicine shows selling 'a cure what ails you' in a bottle to anyone who was gullible enough to fall for their lines. It was claimed that they often had some who would be paid to testify to the healing properties of their potion. As a result, the term 'snake oil' became used metaphorically for any product with exaggerated marketing but questionable benefits.

"Something is rotten in Denmark"

William Shakespeare, Francis Bacon, John Florio, Edward de Vere (17th Earl of Oxford), or whoever actually wrote the famous Shakespearean plays can get credit for this, because it is from *Hamlet*. The officer Marcellus, having just seen the ghost of Hamlet's father, the late King of Denmark, blurts out. "Something is rotten in the state of Denmark!" This has come to mean, 'something is definitely wrong here.'

Title page from 1605 printing of Hamlet

"SOS"

Most people think that SOS means 'save our ships,' or possibly 'save, oh, save.' Another popular belief is that it was originally 'save our souls.' All are wrong.

Here is the real scoop. SOS, the international distress signal for ships, was chosen because of the significance of dashes and dots made for these particular letters in Morse code and is known as a 'prosign,' from 'procedural signal.' All prosigns are transmitted without interletter gaps noted with an 'overbar.' S is three dots, and O is three dashes. Thus, since no gaps are noted, three dots, three dashes and three dots could actually represent other letter combinations in Morse code.

In reality, three of anything, according to expert Fred Bland, is a signal of distress. The signal used before SOS was CQD according to Mark Brader. The regular calling signal was CQ, plus D, representing distress. According to Brader, in 1912 when the Titanic was sinking, the signal sent out was CQD. According to Thomas Hamilton White, the current signal evolved from SOE, but since the last letter was a single dot, it was 'modified to be more distinctive and symmetrical.'

"Sowing wild oats"

This is another of those phrases used today which most people would not suspect was passed down to us by a Protestant preacher, and what's even more surprising, it is from the sixteenth century. The phrase appears in one of Thomas Beccon's tracts from 1542, and a similar expression is credited to the Roman, Plateus.

Wild oats are inferior to the cultivated variety, and are difficult to rid from a field once they are present. Sowing one's wild oats has come to symbolize the youthful tendency toward promiscuity and unprofitable activities. It is often said that young men 'have to sew their wild oats,' much like saying, 'boys will be boys' (see) of younger males. It can be taken as an excuse for misbehaving and a lack of parental guidance for them to overcome the desires to rebel against authority.

"Spill the beans"

In ancient Greece, voting was held by dropping beans into a container. A white bean meant you were for the candidate, a black or dark bean was a 'no' vote. Only the officials could empty the beans and determine the winner.

Occasionally a clumsy voter would knock over the container, spilling the beans, and reveal the results prematurely.

Today spilling the beans means revealing any secret before its time. Pretty cool, huh?

"Square meals"

In medieval times, a dinner plate was a square piece of wood, called a trencher, or square. People always took their 'square' with them when they went traveling, in hopes of getting a square meal.

"Start from scratch"

Starting from scratch is beginning a task without any preparation or advantage. I often said the best cakes are *made* from scratch, joking about how good scratch must be. But the origin of this oft-used phrase has nothing to do with preparing tasty pastries, and doesn't mean 'made form scratch' or basic ingredients.

'Starting from scratch' means starting 'from square one' when everything else has failed.

This saying began being used in the late nineteenth century, but the word 'scratch' has been in use since the eighteenth century when applied to the line drawn on the ground for the starting point of sporting events. The first such scratch had to do with cricket in England, as the boundary line for the batsman. In John Nylon's *Young Cricketer's Tutor*, 1833, he mentions this line from a 1778 work of Cotton:

> "Ye strikers... Stand firm to your scratch, let your bat be upright."

'Scratch,' 'mark' and 'line' became used later as the starting point for races and other athletic events (see 'toe the line').

The Fort Wayne Gazette, in April of 1887, contains what may be the first printed reference to "Starting from scratch," in relation to a cycling race.

> "It was no handicap. Every man was qualified to and did start from scratch."

"stitch in time saves nine, A"

This is one I heard a lot growing up. The origin of this proverb is simply what the wording suggests and nothing more overt, as some have suggested. The phrase is of old Anglo-Saxon origin and spoke of sewing up a hole in fabric before it became larger. This principle was first recorded in Thomas Fuller's *Gnomologia, Adages, Proverbs, Wise Sentences and Witty Sayings, Ancient, Modern, Foreign and British,* 1732.

"A stitch in Time May save nine."

"Stink to high heavens"

This common phrase is likely, like 'Something is rotten in Denmark,' to have originated with the similar saying in *Hamlet*. The afore-mentioned uncle, the King of Denmark, uttered:

"O, my offense is rank, it smells to heaven; It hath the primal eldest curse upon it, A brother's murder."

It is of note that this did not refer to an odor, but to a deed. In recent times the phrase is applied in its current form to actual foul odors.

"Stop and smell the roses"

It seems a bit ironic for this to follow 'stink to high heavens.' I assure you, it was quite coincidental.

Used as a gentle reminder that a friend or family member needs to take time away from a whirlwind work schedule to relax and enjoy the simple pleasures of life, the origin of the saying is a bit cloudy.

It is believed by some to have its beginning in the United States, perhaps a hundred years or so ago. A tale is told of a lady who was an avid rose gardener, so engrossed in her work that she took no time for herself. A dear concerned friend told her that she should take time to stop long enough to enjoy the fruit of her labor by 'smelling the roses.'

In the early 1980s, former Beetle, Ringo Starr, recorded an album with this cliché as its title.

"Straight from the horse's mouth"

This is a saying when a person wants to know the real story, not hearsay. This started because a horse's age can be determined by examining its teeth. It was said that a horse dealer may lie to you but you can always find out the truth 'from the horse's mouth.'

"Straight laced"

Ladies of centuries gone by wore corsets, or a forerunner of a girdle, which would lace up in the front. A proper and dignified woman wore a tightly-tied lace. Thus such a woman, who is likely straight-faced as well, is now called 'straight laced.'

"Strong as an ox"

This idiomatic expression is centuries old and goes back to Old French, Old Greek and Old Latin. Its thoughts were passed down in the tale of Paul Bunyan, who was said to utilize a blue ox named Babe. Oxen have been used by many civilizations as a beast of burden because of their great size and strength. It would make sense to describe someone who was exceed-ingly stout as 'like an ox.'

T

"Take it with a grain of salt"

This common phrase means that one should consider the source of some new 'truth' before swallowing it 'hook line and sinker' (see that little goodie, too).

This has been around since the seventeenth century, and comes from the fact that food is more easily swallowed if taken with a small amount of salt. Pliny the Elder (actually Gaius Plinius Secundus, 23 AD to 25 August 79 AD) translated an ancient antidote for poison with the words 'to be taken fasting, plus a grain of salt.'

"Thank God it's Friday!"

Remember the six day work week? After the formation of the five-day work week in the US, the anticipation of the upcoming weekend at the close of the day on Friday sent a frenzy of happy feelings down the spines of American workers, particularly. Like a wave, when this saying came into being, in the 1960s people utilized it. It soon became shortened to TGIF.

The saying almost immediately spawned the name of a bar and grill called TGI Fridays, which first opened in Manhattan's Upper East Side in 1965. This rapidly became a meeting place for professionals and students in the area, and spread across the country, making the saying TGIF blossom even more in pop culture.

In 1978, a disco movie (first released in the Netherlands) called *Thank God it's Friday*, starring Donna Summer, took the saying to 'fever pitch.' Then in the '90s, ABC TV called their Friday night comedy line up 'TGIF,' in an effort to help families catch the fever.

"That don't make me no never mind"

Okay, okay, so you've never heard this one. Yep. It means, of course, it doesn't make any difference to me, and is poor English at best. I have to admit, it's a US Deep-South mountain expression through and through. But in the South, from the Ozarks to the Appalachians, folks have said this for a number of years. So much so that it has made its way into pop culture in movies and TV shows. It likely started about the 1970's, but has been prevalent over the past three decades in these areas among younger people. Where the idea came from is hard to trace. But I guess it really 'don't make no never mind' anyhow.

"That'll cost you an arm and a leg"

In early America, there were, of course, no cameras. One's image was either sculpted or painted. Some paintings of George Washington, for example, showed him standing behind a desk with one arm behind his back, while others showed both of his legs and both arms. Prices charged by painters of the day were not based on how many people were to be included, but by how many limbs were to be painted. Arms and legs are 'limbs', therefore painting them would cost the buyer more. Hence the expression, "Okay, but it'll cost you an arm and a leg."

This was because hands and arms are more difficult to paint.

"That's all she wrote"

The true origin of this saying has been largely debated. It is thought to have originated from one particular incident involving something written by a woman to a man, though it seems impossible to pin down. It is equated with other popular phrases like, 'that's all there is to it,' and 'that's the end of it.'

There is a popular belief that this saying referred to the 'Dear John letters' written by the girlfriends of servicemen during World War II, which informed them that they had found someone else, and would not still be there with open arms upon their return. This certainly seems feasible. It is said that when the soldiers were asked what else their sweetheart said in the letter, they replied sadly, "That's all she wrote."

The phrase has come to mean anything that is over, and undeniably unrevivable.

"That's the ticket!"

This idiom dates back at least to the early nineteenth century, and means "That's just what is needed." The phrase hasn't changed since it first appeared in print in 1838 in *The clockmaker, or, the sayings and doings of Samuel Slick of Slickville* by Thomas Haliburton:

"They ought to be hanged, sir, (that's the ticket, and he'd whop the leader)."

Thomas Haliburton

However it was brought to life in *NBCs Saturday Night Live,* by Jon Lovitz' character, Tommy Flanagan, in the 1980s. But the use of the word 'ticket' to mean 'the right thing' also spawned the sayings 'Just the ticket,' also dating back to the 1800s.

One theory is that it is a corruption of the French phrase, *"c'est l'étiquette,"* meaning that's the proper thing or course of action.

Another meaning of 'ticket' popular since the seventeenth century is 'a guarantee of some good thing' prompting other phrases like 'You can write your own ticket.'

"There, but for the grace of God, go I"

This saying, used in modern day vernacular by believers and unbelievers in Christianity, has been in common usage since at least the mid twentieth century. It means that should circumstances have taken a different course, anyone could have ended up in a horrible situation. Any of us could have been a criminal, homeless or terminally ill.

The coinage of the phrase is uncertain, with early tribute going to sixteenth century evangelist John Bradford, who was, himself, later burned at the stake in 1555. This credit was propagated by claims that an early edition of *The Oxford Dictionary of Quotations* carried it. If this was true, it had removed the reference by the mid nineteenth century. The saying is nowhere found in the exhaustive writings of Bradford which remain.

"There's method in my madness"

There's no mystery to the origin of this saying. It's another from Shakespeare. It comes from *Hamlet*.

> "Though this be madness, yet there is method in it."

It means that there is a reason behind the actions of the person, no matter how senseless it may seem.

"Third time's the charm/third time lucky"

The reason I'm putting these two together like this is that they are intrinsically tied together — one in the US, the other in the UK — the latter being first with the kudos on coining them both.

The whole idea of third time luck goes back to the numerology of past civilizations and the fact that certain numbers were thought to bring good fortune. Even in the *Bible*, the Israelites felt that certain numbers held privilege with God — the number three being one of them.

The first mention I know about in the English language, and the forebear of the British cliché, 'third time lucky' is again from Shakespeare in *The Merry Wives of Windsor*, *Act V, Scene I (1602)*:

> "Pr'thee, no more prattling: — go. I'll hold: this is the third time; I hope good luck lies in odd numbers. Away, they say there is divinity in odd numbers, either in nativity, chance or death. — Away."

And though the 'charm' version seems only in use in America, in *The Cabinet Album*, by Lewis B. Wayne, 1830, from England, we find:

> "Jack," says he, striving to make himself speak pleasant to him, "you've got two difficult tasks over you; but you know the third time's the charm — take care of the next."

Then, but three years later, in *The Port Admiral*, by William Johnstoun Neal, 1833:

> "Once more they struck it, and splinters of the oak fell among them; but it yielded not.

'Third time's lucky, now again." — but no, it remained firm."

Both gentlemen likely had read the line from Shakespeare.

Three in one explanation:

"Mind your own bee's wax!"

As noted in the 'big wig' explanation, personal hygiene in the olden days was often poor. As a result, many persons, both women and men, had developed acne scars before they reached maturity. The women would apply bee's wax to their faces to smooth out their complexions. When they were talking to one another, if a woman began to stare at another woman's face she was told, 'mind your own bee's wax.'

Now it is humorously used for 'mind your own business.'

"Crack a smile"

Should a woman smile, the bee's wax on her face would crack, hence the term 'crack a smile.' This now means, begin a simper.

"Losing face"

In addition, when they sat too close to the fire, the wax would melt. Therefore, the expression 'losing face' came to be. Losing face is used to indicate declining in popularity or honor in the eyes of others.

"Three may keep a secret, but two of them are dead"

Yep, another one from Ben Franklin's *Poor Richard's Almanac*. If we would all think about the results of divulging information secrets would not get into the hands of the enemy (see "Loose lips sink ships"). Even what we say in emails and on the phone is not guaranteed to stop there any more.

"Throw in the towel"

This one's not difficult to figure out. It is a boxing expression going way back to the early days of professional prizefighting. Many times the boxer couldn't get to his feet when the bell rang signaling the next round was beginning. If the manager knew the boxer was too weak to continue, they would throw in the towel that was used to wipe up blood, signifying surrender.

This adage now has the same connotation as the towel in days of old — quit while you still can, before the end result is worse.

"Till the cows come home"

Cows will be cows. They will take their sweet time coming back to the barn — unless they are dairy cows needing to be milked. But cows in general were the premise of this saying, which has been with us since who knows when — at least the early nineteenth century. The place of origin could have been Scotland. It first appeared in print in January 1829 in *The Times*.

> "If the Duke (of Wellington) will but do what he unquestionably can do, and propose a Catholic Bill with securities, he may be Minister, as they say in Scotland 'until the cows come home.'"

In the 1933 film, *Duck Soup*, Groucho Marx, in his normal dry, straight-faced humor, made the statement:

"I could dance with you till the cows come home. Better still, I'll dance with the cows and you come home."

The saying seems no less popular today, and means for an undetermined, likely *lengthy* period of time.

"To boot"

Getting something 'to boot' means you get it in addition to the product or service bargained for. The term is a corruption of the Old English word *bot*, which meant profit or advantage.

"Toe the line"

Toeing the line is conforming to an established standard. Demanding that one do so is a requirement for some agendas, both occupationally and politically.

This originated from placing one's toes in a strategically important position at or behind a line, scratch or mark for the beginning of a race, toe-to-toe prizefight or any other athletic competition. This practice was common in the nineteenth century in Britain, Scotland and Ireland, and for those immigrants who came over the Atlantic to America who had been accustomed to the practice in their native homeland. Thus, it may have been stated, "toe the mark," or whatever was being toed. When applied to the boxing matches, anyone capable of competing was said to be 'up to scratch.' This is also the origin of the saying 'start from scratch' (see).

In *The Diverting History of John Bull and brother Jonathan*, 1813, by 'Hector Bull-us,' a pen name used by James Paulding, the earliest known reference in print, 'mark' is the word used.

> "He began to think it was high time to toe the mark."

Obviously, the connotation here is figurative already, at this early date, rather than literal.

"To give someone the third degree"

I can tell you the origin of this idiom with my eyes blindfolded — pun intended. This phrase is derived from the ritual in the Freemasons, having been conducted since the eighteenth century, of granting degrees upon members of the fraternity who have earned them. The third degree is an especially grueling one, in which the Lodge Brother is blindfolded, led through the lodge in a prescribed manor, questioned at length, and warned not to divulge the secrets to which they have been made a party by virtue of their degree. The ceremony can last up to forty-five minutes, and is so intense that 'giving someone the third degree' has come to be synonymous with telling a person very sternly what they should or should not do. The term has also come to apply to a harsh interrogation given by law-enforcement agencies

"To have a friend, be a friend"

This is a spin-off saying from the Golden Rule, 'Do unto others as you would have them do unto you' (see). When I thought about including this proverb, it brought to mind the old tale about the happy young couple from the city who were thinking of moving to the Midwestern US farm country to start a family. As they drove leisurely through country along the verdant grassy meadows, they observed a farmer out mowing the hay.

The man pulled their car over and hollered out to the farmer "Hello there, sir. How are the people around here for neighbors?"

"How are the people where you folks live now?" he asked.

"Oh," replied the man in the car, "we have great neighbors now. They watch our house when we are away, and feed our dog. They are honest and dependable."

"Well," said the old farmer, "you'll find them pretty much the same around here."

About a year later, the same farmer was out again, driving a cow to the barn for milking. Another car pulled over, and a straight-faced man with wrinkled brow emerged, waving him over to the fence.

"I was thinking of moving here from the city," he said. "How are people around here to get along with?"

"How are they where you come from?" the farmer asked.

"Oh, can't get along with any of them," he snapped. "Bunch of idiots. Can't trust anybody around there. I'm looking to get around some better people."

"Well, you'll find them pretty much the same around here," the farmer returned.

"To pull strings"

If you've ever had anyone use their influence for you to get a job, or change someone's opinion, then you know what it means to get someone 'to pull some strings' for you, so to speak.

This idiom goes back to the seventeenth century, and was coined from the old days of stringed marionettes. The man behind the curtain pulled the puppet's strings or manipulated him or her to make the show happen. The *American Heritage Dictionary of Idioms,* page 517, gives the following as 'from the first half of the 1800s,' but offers no source:

> "His father pulled some strings and got him out of jail."

"Tried and true"

This is originally a woodworking term. A try plane is used to create a flat surface on a piece of wood being leveled. When the surface has reached the desired state of perfection, it is said to be 'true.'

Tried and true as an idiom means that something has been proven to be the right way of doing or thinking 'beyond the shadow of a doubt' (see). Usually, this refers to methods of accomplishing a desired result which culminates in success.

"Turn the other cheek"

This saying is a quote from Jesus in his famous 'Sermon on the Mount,' and is found in both *Matthew 5:39* and the parallel scripture in *Luke 6:29*. In the King James Version, 1611, the Matthew reference reads like this:

> "But I say unto you, That ye resist not evil: but whosoever shall smite thee on thy right cheek, turn to him the other also.".

Jesus' teaching was so contrary to that of 'an eye for an eye and a tooth for a tooth' in the

Torah (*Exodus 21:24*) taught by the Jewish leaders of the day that he was hated by them, which ultimately led to his crucifixion.

This saying has become a cliché which is frequently used on television and in movies, and has become a part of our general jargon. Often it is used in the negative sense, such as 'I'm not very good at turning the other cheek.'

"Two heads are better than one"

Though not specifically saying 'heads,' the root of this clever proverb goes all the way back to the *Bible*. Its first appearance in English was in the *Miles Cloverdale Bible published in 1535, Ecclesiastes 34:9:*

"Therfore two are better then one, for they maye well enioye the profit of their laboure."

In John Heywood's *Dialogue conteinyng the momber in effect of all the prouerbes in the English tongue*, 1546, we find the first English notation of a close form of the proverb in this entry:

"Some heades haue taken two heades better
then one:
But ten heades without wit, I wene as good
none."

In this reference, head means 'mind.' The
meaning of the saying is that when two
thinkers combine their ideas, often the result is
more profound than those of one alone.

U

"Under the gun"

This phrase is one in which the origin was quite literal. It came from the bygone days in which fortresses and castles armed with artillery were besieged by enemies. When the siege took place, the final step was to throw infantry against the broken walls and into the artillery battery on the solid walls remaining.

The attacking artillery was therefore 'under the gun' to complete the attack in a prompt manner.

Today anyone who is put 'between a rock and a hard place' (see) and forced to act quickly is said to be 'under the gun.'

"Under the weather"

This is an age-old expression which derived from the days when all travel outside the boundaries of land was done on passenger ships. On cross-oceanic voyages, sea sickness was common. In the midst of a harsh storm, passengers would go below deck to be 'under the weather.' Another application was the nautical term, 'under the weather bow,' which is below the sharp end of the ship, and takes the brunt of the storm. Those passengers traveling there would tend to get even sicker.

Today the term is used to indicate any type of sickness or discomfort.

"Ups and downs"

Ups and downs represent a mix of good and bad experiences in life, something to which every human can relate. As an idiom, this phrase has been around in America for many years. I know that it has been actively used for at least the past one hundred years.

The first mention I have found was the title of a 1915 movie featuring Oliver Hardy.

The term can also apply to moodiness. A person with what is now known as 'bipolar disorder' experiences an inordinate amount of mood swings, or 'ups and downs' in their behavior patterns.

Other films and television have also used the name.

The mood of our modern age has brought a lot of attention to the thought of 'Ups and Downs.' At least six current music artists have recorded songs or albums with this theme.

"Upset the applecart"

In the late nineteenth century, 'applecart' was wrestling slang for 'body'. To upset one's applecart was to throw them down.

Through the years it has come to mean that someone's plans have been foiled.

"Up the creek without a paddle"

This is the clean version of a World War II saying meaning to be in one whale of a pickle. There is an earlier version, however, which, according to *Heavens to Betsy! & Other Curious Sayings*, 1955, page 187, goes back as far as 1884, to the political campaign song, "Blaine, Up Salt Creek." A 'salt creek' leads through a salt marsh, or marshland to the ocean. It is very easy to get stuck in one of these babies without a paddle. Not something a political candidate would look forward to.

V

"Va-va-voom!"

This exclamation possibly dates back to the 1950s. It was the title for a piece of music by jazz composer Gil Evans used in a movie in 1985 called *Absolute Beginnings* based on a 1959 novel.

It was made famous by French football star Thierry Henry, and then utilized by Renault, a French auto maker, in an ad campaign in the UK. It is now included in *The Oxford Dictionary of the English Language*.

They define the phrase without reservation to mean just what it has come to be in modern late-twentieth and early twenty-first century slang—'the quality of being exciting, vigorous and attractive.' It has gone far past merely being applied to Renault, or any other automobile with good looks and fast acceleration. The phrase is used particularly by men to express the attractiveness and sex appeal of women.

"Vanish into thin air"

It was good ole Will Shakespeare who gave us the roots of this popular cliché. He came within a hair's breadth in *Othello* in 1604.

> "Then put up your pipes in your bag, for I'll fly away; Go, vanish into air; away!"

Then, in 1610, a line from *The Tempest* was almost 'on the money.'

> "These our actors, as I foretold you, were all spirits and melted into air, into thin air."

The term, 'thin air,' coined by Shakespeare, was later used by other authors, such as John Milton and William Blake.

Finally, in April of 1822, *The Edinburgh Advertiser* put it all together in an article about the situation looming between Russia and Turkey.

> "The latest communications make these visions 'vanish into this air.'"

The rest is history.

"Vicious circle"

Also known now as a 'vicious cycle,' this term was used by logicians in the eighteenth century to describe fallacious proof in this form:

A depends on B
B depends on C
C depends on A

It was mentioned in the *3rd Edition* of the *Encyclopedia Britannica* in 1792.

"He runs into what is termed by logicians a vicious circle."

A wider usage of the phrase was taken by the medical profession in the nineteenth century to describe conditions in which one system affects another and the health of the patient steadily deteriorates.

The broader use of this phrase in our day as an idiom can be any situation which seems to follow a continuous downward spiral, never improving.

W

"Waiting in the wings"

As long as theaters have existed, actors who were awaiting their cue to enter from 'stage left' or 'stage right' have waited in the wings. This phrase has become a metaphor for all who wait patiently for opportunity to knock for them to play their parts in the drama of life. I can locate no first usage of this, but suspect it has been used in the literal sense a very long time, indeed.

Diana Ross had a hit recording titled *Waiting In the Wings*, written by Peter Sinfield and Andy Hill, and released by Motown in 1992. Its chorus rang out:

> "When your heart is weary
> When you want a love with no strings
> I will be here waiting
> Waiting in the wings."

On the Origin of the Clichés & Evolution of Idioms

"Walking on eggshells"

The exact origin of this phrase is unknown, but most agree that it is from an earlier expression, 'walking on eggs.' It means that one is having to be extremely cautious not to upset another person or persons in reference to a particular topic or matter due to the person's sensitivity about it. Other such expressions are 'walking on thin ice' and 'walking on broken glass.'

"Weasel out of"

This colloquialism originated in the mid 1950s, and is based on the stealthy hunting and nesting habits of the slender, sneaky weasel.

'Weaseling out of' a duty or job assigned or expected of someone means 'find a way to avoid doing it.'

"Welcome as flowers in May"

Sometimes now 'welcome as the flowers in springtime,' this was originally printed in *A Hand-book of Proverbs*, by John Ray first published in London, England in 1670.

It is used freely to tell people in a pleasant way that they are appreciated and that what you do for them is done freely—not because you expect something in return.

"Wet behind the ears"

This phrase had its origin in the United States in the early twentieth century. All farmers were accustomed to the helplessness of baby animals, which are naturally wet at birth. When the little one begins to dry, the areas behind the ears are usually last to dry, causing the saying, 'it's still wet behind the ears.'

As per usual, this saying soon came to represent the helplessness and naiveté of beginners when trying to learn new skills. Someone who is 'still wet behind the ears' is either just learning, or this may be applied to a young boy, who seems to know nothing of life's complexities. At any rate, the person so evaluated has a lot to learn.

The earliest known printed reference is in the *Portsmouth Daily Times* (Ohio) in October 1941.

"There is not much in the matter so far as the organ [the courthouse record] is concerned except it is so new that it is wet behind the ears yet."

"What goes around comes around"

There is a printed reference to this phrase in the US in Eddie Stone's book, *Donald Writes No More*, 1974, but the roots are much older. It became popular in America around that time.

I read on *The Phrase Finder* that a much older version, being used in Virginia, possibly in the nineteenth century, was 'what goes around a horse's back comes around a horse's belly.' I feel that this was likely the basis of the current saying. Some British folk say that it started there, and has been passed down from generation to generation.

Its meaning is something like 'you get what you give' and getting 'a dose of our own medicine' — that whatever we dish out will be dished back.

"What's sauce for the goose is sauce for the gander"

I can still hear my mother saying this to me when I didn't want to do something everyone else was required to do. In the US it has commonly been used to mean what is good for a woman, a man should be willing to do.

The saying in this form goes back to at least 1704, when it was recorded in *Brown's New Maxims,* according to *The Oxford English Dictionary.* An earlier form not using the word 'sauce' was reportedly in use from 1579.

"What the dickens!"

This old saying did not come from Charles Dickens, as some may have thought, but from an ancient name for the devil. This is merely another way of saying 'what the devil.' In fact, Shakespeare used it in *The Merry Wives of Windsor* published in 1602.

> "I cannot tell what the dickens his name is my husband had him of."

'Like the dickens' is also in common usage.

"When it rains it pours"

This saying, per se, was started as a slogan for Morton Salt Company in 1911, and was created by A. W. Ayer and Son, an ad agency hired by Morton to come up with a catchy slogan for their new and improved salt. After rejecting a couple of slogans, this one caught Mr. Morton just right, and it has become a catch-phrase for actual rain showers as well as calamities and unexpected and unwanted surprises which may befall us — when one problem comes, they seem to come in bunches.

But this was not the origin of the thought, which is actually unknown but dates prior to 1726 in the UK, when it was used as the title of a work about a whit bear by John Arbuthnot.

> "It cannot rain but it pours; or London strow'd with rarities."

"When my ship comes in"

I've heard this one all my life, and the origin is about what most folks would expect. In centuries past, in coastal towns a major source of the income of locals was interest in trading companies. When the ship in which they had invested took to sea with cargo, they lived in anticipation of the profit they would be paid when it returned. At that time, all shareholders would be paid their share. Sort of like a farmer running credit based on the harvest. They would pay their debts 'when their ship came in.'

Through the years this phrase came to mean when anyone 'struck it rich' they would fulfill their life's dreams, or purchase something they had long desired. More often than not, however, there was no real source for their hope, and it was like an item on a wish list which would always remain 'pie in the sky' (see).

"When pigs fly"

Well, when this phrase is used, you'll know the speaker has no hope that the matter being discussed will ever reach fruition. At least he or she has a sense of humor.

This current version was not the first. The original saying was recorded in John Withals' Latin American dictionary, *A Short Dictionarie for Younge Begynners* in the section on proverbs, page 593, 1616 Edition only.

"Pigs fly in the ayre with their tayles forward."

This expressed sarcasm and the thought that some folks were exceedingly gullible.

Thomas Fuller, in *Gnomologia,* in 1732, got a bit closer to our present meaning.

"That is as likely as to see an Hog fly."

Then in 1835, in *The Autobiography of Jack Ketch,* by Charles Whitehead, we find:

"Yes, pigs may fly, but they're very unlikely birds."

You get the pig-ture. Like so many others, it has evolved to what it is today. And when pigs fly nothing will change.

"Whole ball of wax"

Boy, there are a bunch of these goodies, like 'the whole shebang,' and 'the whole enchilada.' But let's take first things first. This cookie has been baked so long that it's going for lots of dough.

Until recently, researchers assumed it was from the 1950s. But, nope, it goes lots further back. The earliest found so far is from the *Atlanta Constitution* on 25 April 1882:

> "We notice that John Sherman & Co. have opened a real estate office in Washington. Believing in his heart of hearts that he owns this country, we will be greatly surprised if Mr. Sherman does not attempt to sell out the whole ball of wax under the hammer."

Around that time period there are other printed references in American newspapers to 'the whole ball of wax,' so it would be reasonable to assume that it was already well-known in the late nineteenth century.

However, another, only a few months later, found in the *Indiana Democrat* (Pennsylvania), just prior to the election, has the idiom in quotation marks, apparently indicating that it had been recently coined.

> "The Democrats can beat the 'whole ball of wax' this season."

No one seems to be sure why a ball of wax was used, however there is an old belief that it is a humorous modification of *whole bailiwick*, a word which goes back to the fifteenth century, and can mean 'a special domain' according to the *Merriam Webster Dictionary.*

"Wing and a prayer"

This saying is used to express hopeful doubts of success in an endeavor. In World War I, when a flyer returned despite a badly damaged wing, he reported that he had been praying that he would make it back safely. Afterward it was said that he made it on a wing (the one good one) and a prayer.

"With flying colors"

In olden days, if a country's fleet won a decisive victory over an enemy, the ships would sail back to their home port with their colors proudly flying from their masts. Now this is used to mean an easy win or passing grade.

"With friends like you, who needs enemies?"

Versions of this saying have been around for hundreds of years — even before it was known in the English tongue. The original Latin phrase from which it is derived was: *"Dai nemici mi guardo io, dagli amici mi guardi Iddio!"* The literal translation is: "I (can) protect myself from my enemies; may God protect me from my friends!"

Another old version, which some believe to be the original, is: 'He who has a Hungarian for a friend needs no enemy.' Other nationalities also have such derogatory phrases.

It is used in good-natured jest among friends — usually of the same racial background, and not as a true put-down.

Y

"Yellow-bellied"

For hundreds of years the color yellow has been associated with cowardice and treachery. In ancient France, the doors of traitors' houses were daubed with yellow dye. The medieval 'yellow star' which was later utilized by the Nazis, branded Jews as having 'betrayed Jesus.' In medieval paintings, Judas Iscariot, the ultimate symbol of treason to Christians, was portrayed wearing yellow garments. In Spain, victims of the Inquisition wore yellow clothing to imply that they were guilty of heresy and treason. In the old American West, during the early nineteenth century, anybody thought to be worthless was called a 'yellow-dog.'

The combination of yellow, symbolizing cowardice and treachery, with the belly or 'guts,' representing stamina, grit and heroism, speaks clearly the reason for this catch-phrase. A person with guts is a person with courage. The oxymoron 'yellow-bellied' was thus an obvious way of saying the person had no courage.

'Yellow-belly' began to be used in England as a 'mildly derogatory' nickname in the late eighteenth century. Grose's, *A provencial glossary; with a collection of proverbs, etc.*, 1787, lists this term.

> "Yellow bellies. This is an appellation given to persons born in the Fens, who, it is jocularly said, have yellow bellies, like their eels."

A General Dictionary of Provincialisms, by William Holloway, 1839, also lists this phrase in the same light.

> "Yellow-belly, A person born in the Fens of Lincolnshire (From the yellow, sickly complexion of persons residing in marshy situations)."

The usage of this phrase to describe a coward per se first appeared around 1925 in the US.

"You can lead a horse to water but you can't make it drink"

Here is a real contender for the contest as one of the oldest proverbs in the English language (since the *Bible* was not in English at this date).

That is still in popular use after all of these centuries. It was recorded as early as 1175 in *Old English Homilies.*

> "Hwa is thet mei thet hors wettrien the him self nule drinken? (Who can give water to the horse that will not drink of its own accord?)"

Its implied meaning goes for people — they will only do what they have a mind to do.

"You can't get blood out of a turnip"

Though it has been suggested that this humorous term, often associated with the 'Deep South' of the US, came from the biblical story in *Genesis* in which God refused Cain's offering from his crop in favor of Abel's blood offering from an animal, it is first found in print in 1836. It is from Captain Frederick Marryat in *Japhet, In Search of a Father.*

> "There's no getting blood out of a turnip."

Its meaning now as an idiom is that debtors cannot get money from someone who is indigent. Another less-known phrase is 'you can't get blood out of a stone.'

"You can't teach an old dog new tricks"

All you other old geezers, who believe this, raise your hands. That's what I thought. The actual meaning of this today is supposed to be that younger folks learn more easily, and that's certainly true. This saying, like most animal idioms and proverbs, has been with us for hundreds of years, and has become personified because the similarities between animal and human behavior patterns.

But tell this to a lot of retired folks who learned new skills and crafts and they will beg to differ.

The idea behind this saying has been around since at least the sixteenth century. It was brought down to us by our good friend of proverbs, John Heywood, in his 1546 book. The earliest reference to the idea from which this sprang, however, is from John Fitzherbert in *The boke of husbandry* in 1536.

> "...and he [a shepherd] muste teche his dogge to barke whan he wolde haue hym, to ronne whan he wold haue hym, and to leue ronning whan he wolde haue hym; or els he is not a cunninge shepeherd. The dogge must lerne it, whan he is a whelpe, or

els it will not be: for it is harde to make an olde dogge to stoupe."

'Stoupe' here meant 'put its nose to the ground and find a scent.'

"Young whippersnappers"

Well, y'all, if you don't know what this means, or where it comes from, listen up. I heard it first from such legends as Gabby Hayes, Roy Rogers' 'sidekick' (see).

It all had to do with cowboys and ropin' them thar' steers in the old American West. Since the seasoned ropers had to train the younguns who didn't know diddley squat about stuff like that, they had to train them in the important skills of snappin' the rope and whoopin' up on them steers. They called the trainees 'young whippersnappers.' Well, it just kinda stuck. Now a novice is a 'young whippersnapper.' Ya'll get it?

"Your goose is cooked"

This phrase means that you have done some-thing that you will sorely regret. All hope is gone, and you are now in deep trouble.

One theory of the very early origin of this saying is that in the denizens of a besieged city in the sixteenth century hung out a goose to show their attackers that they were not starving. This so enraged the enemy that they burned the town and cooked the goose. This, however, seems 'silly as a goose' to me.

I prefer to favor the belief that it referred to the 'goose that laid the golden eggs,' which the farmer killed to get the gold inside. Hence, the saying, 'don't kill the goose that lays the golden eggs' (see), meaning do not destroy the one thing that will continue to provide for your needs.

There were references to 'gone goose' as early as 1830, meaning a person beyond hope. One such example that year was in a newspaper called *The Massachusetts Spy*, which printed the phrase, "You are a gone goose, friend."

It seemed that the idea of cooking someone's goose was floating around by 1845. In a South Carolina newspaper, *The Southern Patriot*, on 22

February of that year, the following humorous article appeared:

> "HOW TO COOK YOUR NEIGHBOR'S GOOSE. — Collar him, take a moderate sized stick, hickory will do, stir him up; apply offensive epithets; when he boils over with rage, continue dressing, baste sufficiently, and when he's properly served out, his goose is cooked."

Printed reference to this phrase in the sense we know it dates to England in a ballad published in London in 1851 bemoaning the Pope's appointment of Cardinal Wiseman as Archbishop of Westminster.

> "If they come here we'll cook their goose, the Pope and Cardinal Wiseman."

And this may indeed be the evolution of this familiar idiom.

"Your name is mud (or Mudd)"

This is one not to be taken for granted, no matter what you've heard, so please read it all.

After Abraham Lincoln was assassinated at Ford Theater in Washington, DC, on 'Good Friday' evening, 14th April 1865, his killer, actor John Wilkes Booth, who was in great pain from an injury he sustained in a fall from the stage, and a friend, rode on horseback to the plantation home of Dr. Samuel Mudd. Their arrival was at about 4:00 AM. Dr. Mudd treated Booth and, at daybreak, had a neighbor make a set of crutches for him.

Mudd later denied knowing Booth, but was taken to trial, where testimony was given that they did indeed know each other. Mudd was convicted of treason and sentenced to life in prison. He later confessed to lying to protect his family. He became so nationally hated that someone who is harshly disliked is sometimes told, "Your name is Mudd!"

But, this was not the *true* origin of the popular slang saying, no matter what we think in the US, for it was in circulation long before there was even a President Lincoln, as it was listed by "J. Bee" a pseudonym for John Badcock, in *A Dictionary of the Turf, etc.,* in England in 1823!

> "Mud - a stupid twaddling fellow. 'And his name is mud!' ejaculated upon the conclusion of a silly oration, or of a leader in the Courier."

So, since it was originally 'mud,' not Mudd, where did it originate? We know the composition of mud: dirt and water. Actually, it began to be used figuratively as early as the sixteenth century — that's right, the 1500s — to refer to things which were worthless. It later was applied to people as early as 1703 in the account of London's low-life, *Hell upon Earth*.

"Mud, a Fool or thick skull Fellow."

Then, in the nineteenth century there were many printed examples of 'as fat as mud,' 'as rich as mud,' as sick as mud,' etc. These comparisons, meaning decaying and worthless, were enough to use it with someone's name as an insult. Other sayings such as 'dragged through the mud,' and 'mud in your eye' came along as well as 'your name is mud.'

Now you know, as the late Paul Harvey used to say, "the r-r-est of the story!"

"Your neck of the woods"

This expression was first coined in colonial America to relate to the particular area of the country in which a colonist lived. 'Neck' had been used in the English language since the mid sixteenth century to refer to a narrow strip of land, usually surrounded on three sides by water, because it seemed to resemble the neck of an animal. The early Americans used the word to refer to a narrow stand of timber, or expressly to a settlement formed in a particular section of the woods. Since the countryside was covered with forests, "your neck of the woods" was your neighborhood. Even NBC's *Today Show* weatherman, Al Roker still uses this common Americanism in talking of the weather in the viewers' particular region.

"You scratch my back, I'll scratch yours"

This is a kind of a 'quid pro quo' thing (see); if you do somebody a favor, they'll do one for you. It is of nautical derivation, like a good many of these expressions.

Back in the seventeenth century when this saying was first coined the punishments in the British Navy for being AWOL, drunk or disobeying the orders of your superior were very severe. One method was to tie the disobedient sailor to a mast and require another sailor to flog him with a cat-of-nine-tails. Crew members would make deals between them to only strike the other lightly (merely scratching the other's back), to insure that they would receive the same treatment should the process be reversed.

Z

"Zero tolerance"

This term came into common usage in the United States in the 1970s as a way of enforcing laws against certain crimes for which the federal or state government, company or group involved wanted constituents to know that it would not be tolerated under any circumstances. To enforce the law, extra law-enforcement officials would be assigned to high crime areas in which the problem existed. The first known printed reference to the phrase in this connotation is in the *New York Times* in December of 1972.

> "Federal officials say the calculations were based on 'assuming zero tolerance' from now on for ineligibility and overpayments."

The phrase was in limited use in engineering circles as early as the 1950s. It likely evolved from the name of a precision tool which came into use in the early 1940s called a 'Zero Tol.'

"Zonked out"

This is an Americanism which came into use in the late 1950s and meant to become unconscious as a result of alcohol or narcotic drugs.

It has come as an idiom to mean any form of unconsciousness or exhaustion from any source, including becoming so tired from work or exercise that a person or even an animal falls asleep.

Bibliography

Quotes from and/or references to the following printed or recorded sources, including books, plays, films, radio and television programs, songs, poems, magazines, newspapers, journals, currency and other items were noted:

Dictionaries, Encyclopedias and other Reference Books in Alphabetical Order:

A collection of Scots proverbs, Allan Ramsay; J & M. Robertson, Glasgow, Scotland, 1785

A Complete Collection of Scottish Proverbs, James Kelley; C.C. Larkin, London, England, 1721

A dialogue conteinying the number in effect of all the prouerbes in the Englishe tongue. John Heywood, London, England, 1546

A Dialogue Conteynyng Prouerbes and Epigrammes, John Heywood, London, England, 1562

Adagia, Erasmus, (third volume of his Latin proverbs), Venice, Italy, 1508

A Dictionary of Catch-phrases: British and American, from the Sixteenth Century to the

Present Day, Paul Beale, Eric Partridge; Dorsett Press, New York, NY; UK, 1988

A Dictionary of the Turf, "J. Bee", pseudonym for John Badcock, page 98, London, England, UK, 1823

A General Dictionary of Provincialisms, William Holloway, London, England, UK 1839

A Hand-book of Proverbs, John Ray, London, England, 1670.

A New Dictionary of the Terms Ancient and Modern of the Canting Crew, B.E., Gent, London, England, 1698

A provencial glossary; with a collection of proverbs, etc., Francis Grose, London, England, UK, 1787

A Short Dictionarie for Younge Begynners, John Withals, Latin American dictionary, Section on Proverbs, page 583, England, 1616 Edition

Cassell Dictionary of Slang, Jonathon Green; Wingfield and Nicholson, London, UK, 2000

Dictionary of Clichés, James Rogers; Ballantine Books, New York, NY, USA, 1985, 1986

Elegies, Sextus Propertius, Ancient Rome, date unknown

Encyclopedia Britannica, 3rd Edition, Edinburgh, Scotland, 1792

Facts on File Dictionary of Clichés, Second Edition, edited by Christine Ammer; Checkmate Books, New York, NY, USA, 2006

Gnomologia, Adages, Proverbs, Wise Sentences and Witty Sayings, Ancient, Modern, Foreign and British, Thomas Fuller, MD, London, England, 1732

Glossographia, Thomas Blount, London England, 1656

Heavens to Betsy & Other Curious Sayings, Charles Earle Funk; Harper & Row, New York, NY, USA, 1955 (other printings available)

John Cotgrave's English treasury of wit and language and the Elizabethan Drama, Sir John Cotgrave, Gent; Gerald Eades Bentley, London, England, 1655

London Review of English and Foreign Literature, W. Kenrick, London, England, 1767

New Language of Politics; An Anecdotal Dictionary of Catchwords, Slogans and Political Usage, First Edition, William Safire; Random House, New York, NY, USA, 1968

New Maxims, Thomas Brown, England, c.1704

New Song on New Similes, John Gay, England, 1732

Old English Homilies, 1175; reproduced by Early English Text Society, London, UK, 12-3-1998

Paramoigraphy, a book of proverbs, James Howell, London, England, 1659

Richard Taverner's Interpretation of Erasmus' Proverbs, Richard Taverner, London, England, 1545

The American Heritage Dictionary of Idioms, Christine Ammer; Houghton Mifflin Harcourt, Boston, MA, USA, 1997

The Cambridge Dictionary of American Idioms, Paul Heacock; Cambridge University Press, Cambridge, UK, 2003

The Dictionary of American Slang, Originally published in 1960; Collins Reference, 3 Sub Edition, New York, NY, USA, 1998

The Encyclopedia of Word and Phrase Origins; Printed by members of the Norman Society, London, England, UK, 1906

The Facts on File Encyclopedia of Word and Phrase Origins, Robert Hendrickson, Revised Updated Edition; Checkmark Books, New York, NY, USA, 2000

The first tome or volume of the Paraphrase of Erasmus vpon the newe testament, Nicholas Udall's First English translation; Whitchurch, Edward, London, England, 1548

The flowers of wit, or a chance collection of bon mots, Henry Kett; Lackington Allen, and Co., London, England, UK, 1814

The Oxford Dictionary of Proverbs; Oxford University Press, New York, NY, USA, 1998

The Oxford English Dictionary (OED), Second Edition, Version 4.0; Oxford University Press, New York, NY, USA, 2009

The Pocket Magazine of Classics and Polite Literature, John Arliss, London, England, UK, 1832

The Random House Dictionary of Popular Proverbs and Sayings. Gregory Y. Titelman; Random House, New York, NY, USA, 1996

The Underworld Speaks, Albin J. Pollock's directory of slang; Prevent Crime Bureau, San Francisco, CA, USA, 1935

Vocabulum, or The Rogue's Lexicon, George W. Matsell; The Lawbook Exchange, Ltd., London, UK, 2005

Why You Say It, Garrison Webb; Rutledge Hill Press, Nashville, TN, USA, 1992

Wordsworth Book of Euphemism, Neaman, Judith S. and Silver; Carole G. Wordsworth Editions, Hertfordshire, UK, 1995

Films, TV and Radio in Alphabetical Order:

Absolute Beginnings, Directed by Julien Temple; Palace Productions, Buckinghamshire, UK, 1985

A Damsel in Distress, from the novel and screenplay by P.G. Wodehouse, starring Fred Astaire, Joan Fontaine, George Burns and Gracie Allen, Ira Gershwin musical directed by George Stevens; R.K.O. Pictures, Hollywood, CA, USA, 1937

Big Sky Howard Hawks Western film; R.K.O. Radio Pictures, Hollywood, CA, USA, 1952

Blazing Saddles; Mel Brooks; Warner Brothers, Hollywood, CA, USA, 1974

Boys Will be Boys, comedy film, William Beaudine, London, UK, 1935

Chinatown; Robert Evans; Paramount Pictures, Hollywood, CA, USA, 1974

Dr. Strangelove; Stanley Kubrick; Columbia Pictures, Hollywood, CA, USA, 1954

Duck Soup; directed by Leo McCarrey, starring Groucho Marx; Paramount Pictures, Hollywood, CA, USA, 1933

Easy Come, Easy Go; film based on a play by Owen Davis, Directed by Frank Tuttle; Paramount Famous Lasky Corporation, Hollywood, CA, USA, 1928

Easy Come, Easy Go; Hal Wallis, Elvis Presley; Paramount Pictures, Hollywood, CA, USA, 1967

Good Will Hunting; written by Ben Affleck, Matt Damon, directed by Gus Van Sant produced by Lawrence Bender; Miramax Films, Hollywood, CA, USA, 1997

Inherit the Wind; starring Spencer Tracy, Frederick March and Gene Kelley; Universal Studios, Hollywood, CA, USA, 1960

Keeping up with the Joneses; short b/w silent film on Women's style; Gaumont, Hollywood, CA, USA, 1928

Keeping up with the Kardashians; Reality TV series, Kim Kardashian, Eliot Goldberg, Jeff Jenkins; E! Calabasas, CA, USA, 2007-

Lifeboat; from the novel by John Steinbeck, produced by Alfred Hichcock, directed by Kenneth Macgowan; distributed by 20th Century Fox, Hollywood, CA, USA, 1944

Meet the People; Arthur Freed, E.Y. Harburg; M.G.M., Hollywood, CA, USA, 1944

Music Man; Rogers and Hammerstein, Hollywood, CA, USA, 1962

Rio Bravo; Howard Hawks Western; Warner Brothers, Hollywood, CA, USA, 1959

Saturday Night Live; NBC, Hollywood, CA, USA, 1980s episodes

Second Chance / Boys Will be Boys, American TV sitcom, David W. Duclon and Gary Menteer; Fox, Hollywood, CA, USA, 1987-1988

Showgirl in Hollywood, Dir. Mervyn McElroy, Prod. Robert North, Staring Alice White; First National Pictures, WB, Hollywood, CA, USA, 1930

Take It or Leave It, CBS radio quiz show which Hollywood, CA ran from April 21, 1940, to July 27, 1947, and from 1947-1950 on NBC, which changed its title to *The $64 Question* on September 10, 1950 and ran till 1947, Hollywood, CA, USA

TGIF; Friday night 2 hour comedy show; ABCTV, Hollywood, CA, USA, 1988-2005

Thank God it's Friday; disco movie, directed by Robert Klane, starring Donna Summer; Casablanca Filmworks, Motown Productions, Hollywood, CA, USA, Released Netherlands, 1978

The Simpsons TV episode, Hollywood, CA, USA, 1991

The $64,000 Question; TV show1955 to 1958 A spin-off show called *The $64,000 Challenge* was on between 1956 and 1958, Hollywood, CA, USA

The Today Show; Al Roker, meteorologist; NBC TV, New York, NY, USA

The Wizard of Oz; Screenplay, Noel Langdon, Produced by Mervyn LeRoy; MGM, Hollywood, CA, USA, 1939

Twelve Angry Men; Dir. Sidney Lurnet, Pro. Henry Fonda, Reginald Rose, starring Henry Fonda, Lee J. Cobb, E. G. Marshall; United Artists, Hollywood, CA, USA, 1957

Plays in order of initial publication:

Henry VI, William Shakespeare, England, 1591

King John, William Shakespeare, England, 1595

The Merchant of Venice, William Shakespeare, England, 1586

Henry IV, Part II, William Shakespeare, England, 1597

Englishmen for my Money, or *A Woman Will Have Her Will*, Play by William Haughton, London, England, 1598

Julius Caesar, William Shakespeare, England, 1599

Twelfth Night; II, iii, William Shakespeare, England, 1601

Hamlet; William Shakespeare, England, 1602

The Merry Wives of Windsor; Act V, Scene I, William Shakespeare, England, 1602

Othello; William Shakespeare, England, 1604

The Tempest; William Shakespeare. England, 1610

Soddered Citizen; play by Maramion Redux preformed by the King's men at Blackfriar's Theater, cerca 1630

American Abroad; R. B. Peake, two-act comedy, London, England, UK, 1824

A Christmas Carol; Charles Dickens, Chapman & Hall, London, England, UK, 1843

Other Books and Writings in Alphabetical Order:

Absolute Beginnings; Colin MacInnes, novel; MacGibbon & Kee, London, UK, 1959

A Companion to the Temple; Thomas Comber, England, 1676

A Cook's Tale; Geoffrey Chaucer, from *The Canterbury Tales;* Geoffrey Chaucer, England, 1395

A Damsel in Distress; novel by P.G. Wodehouse; George H. Duran, New York, NY, USA, 1919

A Defense of the Ancient Historians; Francis Hutchinson; Powell, Dublin, Ireland, 1734

Adventures of Gil Blas of Santillane; Translator Tobias Smollatt, — translated from the original *L'Histoire de Gil Blas de Santillane* by Alain-Rene Le Sage, Scotland; published anonymously, England, 1750

All round the Wrekin; Walter White; Chapman and Hall, London, England, UK, 1860

A New Home, Who'll Follow, Or Glimpses of Western Life; Mrs. Mary Cleavers (Caroline

Kirkland); Kessinger Publishing, London, England, UK, 1872

A Step from the New World to the old and Back Again; Henry Tappan; Appleton and Co., New York, N.Y., USA, 1852

A work on liberty; Thomas Hobbes, Wiltshire England, 1656

A Young Maid's Fortunes; published that year by Mrs. S. Hall, (Anna Maria Felding) Dublin, Ireland, 1840

Caps for Sale (A Tale of a Peddler; Some Monkeys and Their Monkey Business), Esphyr Slobodkina; Harper Collins, New York, NY, USA, 1987

Certain Tractates; Ninian Winget; William Blackwood and Sons, Edinburgh, Scotland and London, England, 1562

Clarissa, or the History of a Young Lady; Samuel Richardson, London, England, 1748

Conclusion, from *Walden;* Henry David Thoreau; Ticknor and Fields, Boston, MA, USA, 1854

Contemplative Man; Herbert Lawrence; Printed for J. Whitson, London, England, 1771

Country of the Pointed Firs; S. O. Jewett; Haughton Mifflin, Boston, MA, USA, 1896

Defence of the Government of the Church of England; Dr. John Bridges, M. Marprelate, Gent, London, England; written 1587, printed 1588

Donald Writes No More; Eddie Stone; Holloway House, Los Angeles, CA, USA, 1974

Don Quixote; Miguel de Cervantes, Juan de la Cuesta, Spain, 1605, 1615; English translation, 1612, 1620

Dracula, Bram Stoker; Archibald Constable and Company, UK & Republic of Ireland, 1897

Enchiridion Militis Christiani (*Handbook of a Christian Knight*); (first written in Latin 1503-1504), Switzerland, Desiderus Erasmus; English Translation, London, England, 1533

Essayes and characters of a prison and prisoners; Geffray Marshall, England, 1612

Essays on the Intellectual Powers of Man; Thomas Reid, L. White, Dublin, Ireland, 1786

Evelina, or the History of a Young Lady's Entrance into the World; Fanny Burney, Thomas Lowndes, England, 1778

Foure Sonnes of Aymon; William Caxton, translator, Octavia Richardson, Editor, London, England, 1489

Foxes Book of Martyrs; John Fox, London, England, 1570

Garrick's vagary, or, England run mad; with particulars of the Strafford Jubilee; S. Bladon, London, England, 1769, (David Garrick's writings about Shakespeare)

Hell upon Earth; anonymous, London, England, 1703

Hereward the Wake; Charles Kingsley, T. Nelson & Sons, London, England, circa 1035-1072

H. Murray Life & Real Adventures; Hamilton Murray; J. Burr, London, England, 1759

Hollywood Girl, novel by Patrick McEvoy; Simon & Schuster, New York, NY, USA, 1929

Holy Bible – various versions quoted and used as references in order of appearance in the Bible:

On the Origin of the Clichés & Evolution of Idioms

Genesis 3
Genesis 5:21-27
Exodus 21:24
Ezra 6:9
Job 15:7
Job 19:20 Geneva Bible, 1560
Psalms 17:8
Psalms 91:5, Miles Cloverdale Bible, 1535
Proverbs 27:10, New American Standard Version
Ecclesiastes 9:4
Ecclesiastes 10:20
Ecclesiastes 34:9, Miles Cloverdale Bible, 1535
Isaiah 28:23, Miles Coverdale Bible, 1535
Isaiah 40:31
Isaiah 65:5, KJV, 1611
Jeremiah 13:23a
Daniel 5:1-4
Matthew 3:11
Matthew 5:39, KJV, 1611
Matthew 7:12, Miles Coverdale Bible, 1535
Matthew 12:25, KJV, 1611
Matthew 15:14
Luke 6:29
I Corinthians 15:52, KJV, 1611
I Timothy 4:7, KJV, 1611
II Timothy 4:1 Wycliffe, 1385, KJV, 1611

I Couldn't Care Less; Anthony Phelps; Harborough Publishing, London, England, UK, 1946

Indiscretions of Archie; P.T. Wodehouse; Herbert Jenkins, London, England, UK, 1921

Ivanhoe; Sir Walter Scott; A. Constable, London, England, UK, 1820

Japhet, In Search of a Father; Captain Frederick Marryat, England, UK, 1836

Life in Sing Sing; by "Number 1500;" Bobbs-Merrill and Company, Indianapolis, IN, USA, 1904

Major Jones' Courtship; William T. Thompson, Augusta, GA, USA, 1842

Naaman the Syrian, his Disease and Cure; Daniel Rogers, London, England, 1642

Narrative of the life of David Crockett; David Crockett; E.L. Cary and E. Hart, New York, NY, USA, 1834

Narrenbeschwörung (Appeal to Fools); Thomas Murner, Germany, 1512

New Sonnets and Pretty Pamphlets; Thomas Howell, London, England, 1570

Nuttie's Father; Charlotte Mary Yonge (1823-1901); MacMillan, London, England, UK, 1885

On the Origin of the Clichés & Evolution of Idioms

On The Origin of the Species by Means of Natural Selection; Charles Darwin; John Murray, London, England, UK, 1859

Pharmacomastix: Or, the Office, Use, and Abuse of Apothecaries Explained; Charles Lucas, London, England, 1785

Piers Plainnes Seaven Yeres Prentiship; Henry Chettle, London, England, 1595

Plinius Naturalias Historia XXXI; Pliny the Elder Gaius Plinius Secundus (23 AD – August 25, 79 AD0, Rome, 1ST Century AD, English translation, John Bostock and H.T. Riley, London, England, UK, 1855

Plutarch's Lives of the noble Grecians and Romanes; late first century, Plutarch, originally in Greek, Sir Thomas North, English translation, London, England, 1579

Political Ballads; Milton Oswin Percival, London, England, 1731

Racing Maxims and Methods of Pittsburgh Phil; George E. Smith; Casino Press, E.W. Cole, New York, NY, USA, 1908

Reflections on a Flower Garden; James Hervey; J. & J. Rivington, London, England, 1746

Reflections on the Love of God; Lorenzo Dow; J. Borne, Bemersley, England, UK, 1836

Reflections on several of Mr. Dryden's plays; Elkanah Settle; Printed for William Whitwood, London, England, 1687

Remaines of a Greater Worke Concerning Britaine; William Camden, London, England, 1614

St. Ronan's Well; Sir Walter Scott; Archibald, Constable and Co., Edinburgh, Scotland, 1834

School for Scandal; Richard B. Sheridan, London, England, 1777

Second Fruits; John Florio, London, England, 1591

Sketches from Cambridge by a Don; Sir Leslie Stephen; Kessinger Publishing, LLC, London, England, UK, 1865

Stiff Upper Lip, Jeeves; P.G. Wodehouse, London, UK, 1935

The Adventurer; Samuel Johnson and others, page 309; Harrison and Company, London, England, 1793, page 309

The Adventures of Huckleberry Finn; Mark Twain (Samuel Langhorne Clemmons); Chatto & Windus, London, England, UK, 1884

The Antiquary; Sir Walter Scott; Archibald, Constable and Co., Edinburgh, Scotland; Longman, Rees, Orme, Brown and Green, London, England, UK, 1816

The Author's Earnest Cry and Prayer; Robert Burns, Kilmarnock, Scotland, 1786

The Autobiography of Jack Ketch; Charles Whitehead; Carey, Lee and Blanchard, London, England, UK, 1835

The bachelor's banquet; 1603, Thomas Dekker; Vizzetelly & Company, London, England, UK, 1887

The boke of husbandry; John Fitzherbert, London, England, 1534

The Book of Margery Kempe; Jonathan Cape, London, England, written 1438, published 1936

The Bugbears; Francis Kinwelmersh, England, 1580

The Cabinet Album; Lewis Bingley Wayne; Hunt, Chance and Co., London, England, UK, 1830

The Clockmaker, or the Sayings and Goings of Saamuel Slick of Slickville; Thomas Halliburton, Nova Scotia, Canada, 1838; Richard Bentley, London, England, UK, 1839

The Cosmographical Glasse; William Cunningham; John Day, London, England, 1559

The Diverting History of John Bull and brother Jonathan; 'Hector Bull-Us'; Inskeep and Bradford, New York, NY, USA, 1813

The Draft in Baldwinsville; Artemus Ward (Charles Farrar Brown); Harper and Brothers, New York, NY, USA, and London, England, UK, 1862

The Four Last Things; Sir Thomas More, England, 1522

The Friend, a Religious and Literary Journal; Philadelphia, PA, U.S.A., March 10, 1910

The Gentle Craft; Thomas Deloney; Mayer and Muller, Berlin, Germany, 1903

The History of British Work and Labour; Relations in the Royal Dockyards, Routledge, London, England, UK, 1999

The History of Little Goody Two-Shoes; anonymous, London, England, 1765

The Life of P.T. Barnum; autobiography of Phineas T. Barnum, 1855; reprinted by the University of Illinois Press, Chicago, IL, USA, 2000

The Milkmaid and Her Pail; Aesop's fable from 570 BC

The Newcomes; memoirs of a most respectable family; William Makepeace Thackeray; Harper and Brothers, New York, NY, USA, 1857

The Port Admiral; William Johnstoun Neale; Cochrane & McCrone, London, England, UK, 1833

The Prisoner of Azkaban; J.K. Rowling, the Harry Potter series, book 3; Bloomsbury, London, England, UK, 1999

The Rescuing of Romish Fox; Wyllyam Turner; Basyl, London, England, 1545

The Scarlet Letter; Nathaniel Hawthorne; Tickson, Reed and Fields, Boston, MA, USA, 1850

The Wife of Bath's Tale and Prolouge; (now a part of The Canterbury Tales); Geoffrey Chaucer, London, England, 1395

The Works of Jeremy Bentham, Volume IV; page 225, Jeremy Bentham, Edited, John Browning, London, England, UK, 1843

The Young Duke; Benjamin Disraeli; J. & J. Harper, New York, NY, USA, 1831

To Kill a Mockingbird; Harper Lee; J.P. Lippincott and Co., Philadelphia, PA, USA, 1960

Tout vient à qui sait attendre; Violet Fane (Mary Montgomerie Lamb, Baroness Currie) (1843-1905), London, England, UK, circa 1889

Troilus and Criseyde; Geoffrey Chaucer, London, England, 1385

White Monkey; John Galsworthy; C. Scribner's sons, London, England, UK, 1924

Word Myths: Debunking Linguistic Urban Legends; pp. 66-67, David Wilton; Oxford University Press, New York, NY, USA, 2004

Young Cricketer's Tutor; John Nylon, London, England, UK, 1833

Magazines, Journals, Periodicals and News-papers in Alphabetical Order:

Ballou's dollar monthly magazine Volume 5; New York, NY, USA, January 1857

Crawford County Courier; Prairie du Chien, Wisconsin, USA, 1852

Evening State Journal; Lincoln, Nebraska, USA, 1937

Galveston News; Galveston, Texas, USA, 15 August 1954, page 22

Huron Reflector; Norwalk, Ohio, USA, 1830

Iowa Citizen; Iowa City, IA, USA, October 9, 1891

New Hampshire Statesman and State Journal; Concord, Hew Hampshire, USA, August, 1834

New Sporting Magazine; Painting, R. Ackerman, London, England, UK, July 1837

New Yorker Magazine; Peter Arno cartoon illustration, New York, NY, USA, March 1, 1941

Oakland Tribune; Oakland, California, USA, February, 1921

Oxnard Press Currier; Oxnard, California, USA, August, 1946

Poor Richard's Almanac; Benjamin Franklin, Philadelphia, PA, USA, various editions, 1732-1758

Portsmouth Daily Times; Portsmouth, OH, USA, October 1941

Roslin O Roslin; Clan Sinclair Canada publication, *Beyond the Shadow of a Doubt,* Niven Sinclair, Vol. 3, no. 3 and 4, Spring and Summer, 1996

Southern Patriot; pg. 1, Charleston, SC, USA, February 22nd, 1845,

Sporting Life Magazine; Philadelphia, PA, USA, May, 1886

The American Museum Journal; American Museum of Natural History, New York, NY, USA, Volume 3, 1788

The Atlanta Constitution; Atlanta, GA, USA, April 25, 1882, July, 1882

The Berkshire Evening Eagle; Pittsfield, Berkshire, MA, USA, February, 1947

The Boston, Lincoln, Louth & Spalding Herald; newspaper, England, UK, January, 1833

The Boston Morning Post; Boston, MA, USA, 23 March, 1839

The Bridgeport Telegram, Bridgeport, CT, USA, Private Samuel S. Polley, 1918

The Clearfield Progress; Clearfield, PA, USA, newspaper, Cartoon, *'Our Boarding House with Major Hopple,'* 1938

The Daily Currier; Connellsville, PA, USA, November, 1942

The Daily Nevada State Journal; Reno, NE, USA, February, 1876

The Democratic Review; (magazine), New York, NY, USA, 1851

The diary of Sarah Knight in *The Journals of Madam Knight and the Reverend Mister Buckingham,* written in 1704 and 1710, and published in *American Speech,* American Dialect Society, Duke University Press, Durham, NC, USA, 1940

The Dublin University Magazine; Volume 16; Number 92, Dublin, Ireland, January, 1840

The Edinburgh Advertiser; Edinburgh, Scotland, UK, April, 1822

The Edinburgh Magazine; Edinburgh, Scotland, 1787

The Electric Review; monthly periodical, article by William Hendry Stowell, London, England, UK, 1816

The Evening Democrat; Warren, PA, USA, newspaper, October, 1900

The Fort Wayne Gazette; Fort Wayne, IN, USA, April, 1887

The Gentlemen's Magazine; F. Jefferies, London, England, UK, 1770

The Hammond Times; Hammond, IN, USA, 1942

The Illustrated Sporting News; picture of George E. Smith, London, England, UK, October, 1903

On the Origin of the Clichés & Evolution of Idioms

The Indiana Democrat, Indiana, PA, USA, fall, 1882

The Massachusetts Spy, Worchester, MA, USA, June 14, 1815

The Massachusetts Spy, Worchester, MA, USA, article, Isaiah Thomas, 1939

The Middlesex Currier, Middlesex, England, UK, February, 1832

The monthly miscellany; or Gentleman and Lady's Complete Magazine, Vol. II; London, England, UK, 1774

The Nation, Volume 44, number 1146; (a weekly journal), The Evening Post Publishing Co., New York, NY, USA, June 16, 1887

The Newark Daily Advocate, Newark, OH, USA, October, 1900

The Newport Mercury; (newspaper), Newport, RI, USA, June, 1887

The News, Frederick, MD, USA, May, 1942

The New York Gazette and weekly Mercury New York, NY, USA, May 17, 1773

The New York Globe; Keeping Up With the Jonses; Arthur 'Pop' Momand, New York, NY, USA, 1913-1939

The New York Literary Journal; Volume 4; New York, NY, USA, 1821

The New York Magazine; New York, NY, USA, February 15, 1971

The New York Sun; New York, NY, USA, April, 1896

The New York Times; article; New York, NY, USA, August, 1862

The New York Times; New York, NY, USA, ad, 23 October 1862

The New York Times; New York, NY, USA, article, December, 1972

The Olean Evening Times; article by Allene Sumner Olean, New York, NY, USA, March, 1926

The Philadelphia Aurora; article, Philadelphia, PA, USA, 1798

The Post Standard; (newspaper), Syracuse, New York, NY, USA, September 4, 1906

On the Origin of the Clichés & Evolution of Idioms

The Reno Daily Gazette; story, Reno, NV, USA, 1876

The Saturday Evening Post; The Black Cat; short story, Edgar Allen Poe, Philadelphia, PA, USA, August 19. 1843

The Spectator; (newspaper) Richard Steele, London, England, UK, 1711

The Stevens Point Daily Journal; Stephens Point, WI, USA, May, 1909

The Syracuse Herald; article, *'Great Life, Writes Soldier at Camp,'* Private Walter J. Kennedy, Syracuse, NY, USA, June 29, 1918

The Times, article, London, England, UK, January, 1829

The Times Literary Supplement; London News International, London, England, UK, 1908

The Wilkes-Barre Gleaner; article, *'Who'll turn Grindstones, from essays from the desk of Poor Richard and the Scribe,'* Charles Miner, Wilkes-Barre, PA, USA, 1811

The Winnipeg Free Press, Winnipeg, Manitoba, Canada, article on cinematic drama, March, 1944

William & Mary College Quarterly; Williamsburg, VA, published Richmond, VA, USA, 1710

Songs and Albums in Alphabetical Order:

A Sadder but Wiser Girl for Me from *Music Man;* Rogers and Hammerstein, Hollywood, CA, USA, 1962

Catch a Falling Star; Paul Vance, Lee Pockriss, Perry Como; RCA International, New York, NY, USA, 1957

Easy Come, Easy Go; Elvis Presley, Sid Wayne, Ben Wiseman, title song from movie; Paramount, Hollywood, CA, USA, 1967

Easy Come, Easy Go; album and title song (Aaron Baker, Dean Dillon); MCA Records, George Straight, Produced by Tony Brown, Nashville, TN, USA, 1993

Easy Come, Easy Go; (Diane Hildebrand and Jack Keller) Bobby Sherman; Metromedia, Records, Hollywood, CA, USA, 1970

Get up and Bar the Door; traditional Scottish folk song published Scotland, 1776

On the Origin of the Clichés & Evolution of Idioms

I Heard it Through the Grapevine, Norman Whitfield and Barrett Strong, first released by Smokey Robinson and the Miracles; Motown Records, Detroit, Michigan, USA, 1967

It's Alright Ma (I'm Only Bleeding); Bob Dylan; Columbia Records, New York, NY, USA, 1965

My name is Kelly; song by Howard Pease, 1919

Not a Dry Eye in the House, song written by Diane Warren, CD recorded by Meat Loaf; Virgin Records, Ltd., London, UK, 1995

Stop and Smell the Roses; Record album produced by Paul McCartney, George Harrison Harry Nilsson, Ronnie Wood, Stephen Stills, Ringo Starr, sung by Ringo Starr; RCA, London, UK, 1980

Street Ballad, London Labour; H. Meyhew, London, England, UK, 1851

The Preacher and the Slave; folk song by labor activist Joe Hill, USA, 1911

Unanswered Prayers, Garth Brooks, Pat Alger, Pat Bastian, Recorded by Garth Brooks; Capitol Records, Nashville, TN, USA, 1989

Va-va-voom! Gil Evans and his Orchestra, Virgin Records, Ltd., London, UK, 1986

Waiting In the Wings; written by Peter Sinfield and Andy Hill, Diana Ross; Motown Records, Detroit, MI, USA, 1992

When I was a Lad; Gilbert and Sullivan, parody sung by Allan Sherman and Lou Busch; ASCAP, Burning Bush Music, WB Music Corp, Los Angeles, CA, USA, 1963

Poems in Alphabetical Order:

An Essay on Criticism; poem by Alexander Pope (1688-1744), England, 1709

A Select Second Husband; poem by John Daves, England, 1616

A Wife; poem by Thomas Overbury, England, 1613

Comus: A Mask Presented at Ludlow Castle; John Milton, first presented at Michaelmas, Ludlow Castle, Shropshire, England, 1634

Confessio Amantus; (The Lover's Confession) John Gower, narrative poem, England, 1390

On the Origin of the Clichés & Evolution of Idioms

Five Hundreth Poinrtes of Good Husbandrie; instructional poem, Thomas Tusser, London, England, 1573

Generydes, a Romance in Seven Fine Stanzas; anonymous medieval poem, Trinity College Library, Cambridge, England, circa 1440

Hudibra; satirical narrative poem by Samuel Butler, London, England, 1664

Overbury's Wife; Thomas Overbury, England, 1613; published, 1614

Primrose Path; poem by Ogden Nash, 1936

The Babes in the Woods; narrative poem by Rev. Richard H. Barham in *The Ingoldsby Legends;* Thomas Ingoldsby; published London, England, 1856

The Charge of the Light Brigade; Alfred, Lord Tennyson, famous epic poem, London, England, UK, 1864

The Iliad, Homer, Greece, c. 700 BC

The Lay of St. Odille; narrative poem by Rev. Richard H. Barham in *The Ingoldsby Legends;* Thomas Ingoldsby; published London, UK, 1856

The Lost Heir (Long narrative poem); Thomas Hood, England, UK, 1845

The Trial by Existence; Robert Frost, USA, 1915

When Lide Married Him; poem by James Whitcolm Riley, Indianapolis, Indiana, USA, 1894

Work; poem by George Gascoigne, England, 1572

Miscellaneous Sources in Alphabetical Order:

A letter written by first lady Abigail Adams; Massachusetts, USA, dated 13 November 1800

An act for preventing tumults and riotous assemblies, and for the more speedy and effectual punishing the rioters; England, July, 1715

British one pound banknote (notation from)

Handwritten diary of William Richardson; 1815

National Basketball Association (NBA) Playoffs; Son Cook, April, 1978

Notes on the poems of Dryden; Martin Clifford, England, circa 1677

On the Origin of the Clichés & Evolution of Idioms

Occasional Discourse on the Negro Question; Thomas Carlyle, essay; Published in *Frazier's Magazine for Town and Country*), London, England, UK, 1849

Stan Freberg Presents the United States of America: The Early Years; Stan Freberg's comedy album; Capitol W/SW-1573, New York, NY, USA, 1961

Sumner County, Tennessee court records; USA, 1790

The Pied Piper of Hamelin (Legend); (Germany), sixteenth century supposedly happening in 1284

The Selected Letters of Theodore Roosevelt; 1890s first published 1951, edited by H.W. Brands; Rowman & Littlefield Publishers, Lanham, MD, USA, 2007

The Tragedies of the last Age consider'd and examin'd by the Practice of the Ancients, and by the Common Sense of all Ages; in a Letter to Fleetwood Shepheard, Esq. by Thomas Rymer, of Grays-Inn, Esquire, England, 1678

Tract by Thomas Beccon, England, 1542

Which, Right or Left, political article, USA, 1855

Internet Sources:

Information was obtained, paraphrased and searched out from various sections for accuracy, as many items proved to be wrong. Some specific pages used are also noted of the following web sites and blogs, posted as accessed:

General Information sites:

http://www.phrases.org.uk/

http://askville.amazon.com/

http://www.straightdope.com/

http://www.saidwhat.co.uk/phrase-finder/

http://answers.yahoo.com/

http://www.joe-ks.com/phrases/

http://www.jinxiboo.com/blog/

http://en.wikipedia.org/wiki/

http://dictionary.reference.com/

http://www.merriam-webster.com/dictionary/

http://www.clichesite.com/

http://thepartyofthefirstpart.blogspot.com/

http://www.luminarium.org/encyclopedia/

Specific sites:

http://www.bl.uk/learning/langlit/dic/blount/1656blountsglossographia.html

http://www.trivia-library.com/b/origins-of-sayings-damned-if-you-do-and-damned-if-you-dont.htm

http://americaexplained.wordpress.com/2011/02/06/cards-on-the-table/

http://www.associatedcontent.com/article/1932174/snake_in_the_grass_origin_and_meaning.html?cat=37

http://www.tgifriday.com/wordpress/2009/04/03/tgifriday-origin/

http://dictionary.reference.com/

http://grahams-random-ramblings.blogspot.com/2008/09/meaning-and-origin-of-caught-with-his.html

http://users.tinyonline.co.uk/gswithenbank/sayingsg.htm

http://www.wisegeek.com/what-does-it-mean-to-be-walking-on-eggshells.htm

http://www.smh.com.au/news/big-questions/why-the-expression-dog-eat-dog/2005/07/15/1120934399298.html

http://www.worldwidewords.org/qa/qa-hil2.htm

http://www.wordwizard.com/phpbb3/viewtopic.php?f=7&t=20826

https://market.android.com/details?id=book-c1EJAAAAQAAJ

http://www.britannica.com/EBchecked/topic/344735/The-Lives-of-the-Noble-Grecians-and-Romanes

http://www.shakespeare.org.uk/explore-shakespeare/collections/treasures/plutarch-039-s-lives-of-the-noble-grecians-and-romans.html

http://www.goodreads.com/book/show/174
198.The_Country_of_the_Pointed_Firs_and_Ot
her_Stories

http://webcache.googleusercontent.com/searc
h?q=cache:jUX2nc3e1BUJ:www.worldcat.org/t
itle/young-
duke/oclc/2371420+The+Young+Duke,+Benja
min+Disraeli,+J+%26+J+Harper+New+York+1
831.&cd=2&hl=en&ct=clnk&gl=us&source=w
ww.google.com

http://webcache.googleusercontent.com/searc
h?q=cache:97d0Gwu0iHYJ:www.jinxiboo.com
/blog/2009/6/2/freelance-origin-of-the-term-
sir-walter-
scott.html+freelance+quote+Ivanhoe+1820+Sc
ott&cd=3&hl=en&ct=clnk&gl=us&source=ww
w.google.com

http://www.a1outlet.com/SKETCHES-
FROM-CAMBRIDGE-
1865/116486307X/catalog

http://www.pagebypagebooks.com/Charles_
Dickens/A_Christmas_Carol/Stave_1_Marleys
_Ghost_p1.html

http://www.oup.com/us/corporate/contact/
?view=usa

http://www.amazon.com/s/ref=pd_lpo_k2_d p_sr_sq_top?ie=UTF8&keywords=the%20oxfor d%20english%20dictionary%20second%20editi on&index=blended&pf_rd_p=486539851&pf_r d_s=lpo-top-stripe-1&pf_rd_t=201&pf_rd_i=0199563837&pf_rd_m =ATVPDKIKX0DER&pf_rd_r=1DCGCDBF85D K2T2N25MR

http://webcache.googleusercontent.com/searc h?q=cache:B0detlpDii8J:annalwalls.weebly.co m/phrases.html+new+york+literary+journal+ volume+4+1821&cd=7&hl=en&ct=clnk&gl=us &source=www.google.com

http://idiomation.wordpress.com/2011/01/1 9/dont-count-your-chickens-until-your-eggs-are-hatched/

http://www.exclassics.com/hudibras/hbintro .htm

http://books.google.com/books?id=I1rZAAA AMAAJ&pg=PA199&lpg=PA199&dq=ninian+ winget&source=bl&ots=iib_eBKU7k&sig=hRj wJ2hou-kVNe1QGhRwW4qQTv0&hl=en&ei=Cro5TvS 3B8Hd0QGxtZTmCQ&sa=X&oi=book_result& ct=result&resnum=1&sqi=2&ved=0CBkQ6AE wAA#v=onepage&q=ninian%20winget&f=fals e

http://webcache.googleusercontent.com/searc
h?q=cache:TnfIY0jRr-
wJ:www.gwleibniz.com/britannica_pages/era
smus/erasmus.html+Erasmus'+Enchiridion+
Militis+Christiani+1533&cd=7&hl=en&ct=clnk
&gl=us&source=www.google.com

http://riumullit.tk/the-**cosmographical-
glasse**.html

http://www.amazon.co.uk/Couldnt-Care-
Less-Anthony-
Phelps/dp/B002M5EAEI/ref=sr_1_12?s=book
s&ie=UTF8&qid=1312495523&sr=1-12

http://www.online-literature.com/charlotte-
yonge/

http://www.dur.ac.uk/c.e.schultze/works/n
uttie.html

http://www.brassmagazine.com/blog/lexico
n-keeping-joneses

http://www.yourdictionary.com/goatee

http://books.google.com/books/about/A_dic
tionary_of_catch_phrases_American_a.html?id
=077fSAAACAAJ

http://isbndb.com/d/publisher/dorset_press.
html

http://www.amazon.com/Caps-Sale-Peddler-
Monkeys-Business/dp/0064431436

http://www.businessballs.com/clichesorigins.
htm

http://penelope.uchicago.edu/Thayer/E/Ro
man/Texts/Pliny_the_Elder/home.html

http://users.tinyonline.co.uk/gswithenbank/s
ayingsb.htm

http://books.google.com/books?id=MonlAA
AAMAAJ&pg=PA512&lpg=PA512&dq=old+w
warhorse+1653&source=bl&ots=1FyUilD_ss&s
ig=8vmBphHoIxJ4p6NzxyvgZ1DJHfw&hl=en
&ei=lyw_TqbfLarg0QGTnc3pCQ&sa=X&oi=b
ook_result&ct=result&resnum=6&sqi=2&ved=
0CEIQ6AEwBQ#v=onepage&q&f=false

http://www.wordwizard.com/phpbb3/viewt
opic.php?f=7&t=19541&view=previous

http://www.ehow.com/facts_5877431_rotten-
apple-theory.html

http://books.google.com/books?id=2XoEAA
AAQAAJ&printsec=frontcover&source=gbs_g
e_summary_r&cad=0#v=onepage&q&f=false

http://avalon44.tripod.com/

http://webcache.googleusercontent.com/searc
h?q=cache:58pwPzqKlHYJ:www.pages.drexel.
edu/~zk32/clicheorigin.html+ogden+nash+19
36+poem+piece+of+cake&cd=3&hl=en&ct=cln
k&gl=us&source=www.google.com

*http://spenserians.cath.vt.edu/TextRecord.php?actio
n=GET&textsid=33632*

http://webcache.googleusercontent.com/searc
h?q=cache:HWW0uaU3kqoJ:www.newadvent.
org/cathen/05510b.htm+Adagia,+Erasmus,+t
hird+volume+of+his+Latin+proverbs,+1508&c
d=4&hl=en&ct=clnk&gl=us&source=www.goo
gle.com

http://www.emblematica.com/en/cd13.htm

http://colinsghost.org/2010/05/racing-
maxims-and-methods-of-pittsburg-phil-
1908.html

http://www.online-literature.com/poe/24/

http://literaryballadarchive.com/PDF/Barha
m_1_Babes_in_the_Wood.pdf

http://books.google.com/books?id=w9jQ7_A
RwGsC&pg=PA406&lpg=PA406&dq=The+Bu
gbears,+1580&source=bl&ots=l0lIInds81&sig=
3Tha7mvVWDbNwUTzAsrgtr1LZpI&hl=en&e
i=O3VCTpHrL6Le0QG-
p_zdCQ&sa=X&oi=book_result&ct=result&res
num=1&ved=0CBYQ6AEwAA#

http://www.eapoe.org/geninfo/poechron.ht
m

http://books.google.com/books/about/The_
Newcomes.html?id=P-4tAAAAYAAJ

http://books.google.com/books?id=Q44sAAA
AYAAJ&pg=PA16&lpg=PA16&dq=Gnomolog
ia,+Adages,+Proverbs,+Wise+Sentences+and+
Witty+Sayings,+Ancient,+Modern,+Foreign+a
nd+British,+Thomas+Fuller,+1732&source=bl
&ots=M36mWJ6rra&sig=3ECwbQAmczkAtou
4kgaJp3mx028&hl=en&ei=rUJFToLUG8fV0QH
5p7TpBw&sa=X&oi=book_result&ct=result&re
snum=1&ved=0CBYQ6AEwAA#v=onepage&
q=Gnomologia%2C%20Adages%2C%20Prover
bs%2C%20Wise%20Sentences%20and%20Witt
y%20Sayings%2C%20Ancient%2C%20Modern
%2C%20Foreign%20and%20British%2C%20Th
omas%20Fuller%2C%201732&f=false

http://forum.wordreference.com/showthread
.php?t=24038&page=2&pp=10

http://books.google.com/books?id=ImFRAxP
ZmkMC&pg=PA187&lpg=PA187&dq=1884,+t
o+the+political+campaign+song,+%E2%80%9
CUp+Salt+Creek&source=bl&ots=ynJUSLhQS
P&sig=eT-
3kf6TLgWYWCeGeuNJVMFKNyE&hl=en&ei=
U3ZFTr2zHoTn0QGsvYniBw&sa=X&oi=book
_result&ct=result&resnum=3&ved=0CCQQ6A
EwAg#v=onepage&q=1884%2C%20to%20the
%20political%20campaign%20song%2C%20%E
2%80%9CUp%20Salt%20Creek&f=false

http://www.vialibri.net/item_pg/6571415-
1634-withals-john-dictionary-english-and-
latine-devised-for-the-capacitie.htm

http://books.google.com/books/about/The_a
utobiography_of_Jack_Ketch.html?id=86UMA
AAAYAAJ

http://webcache.googleusercontent.com/searc
h?q=cache:GKwPHabriTgJ:www.worldwidew
ords.org/qa/qa-who5.htm+cache:gE-
g8NPZqzIJ:boards.straightdope.com/sdmb/ar
chive/index.php/t-
441841.html+Indiana+Democrat+1882+whole+
ball+of+wax&cd=2&hl=en&ct=clnk&gl=us&so
urce=www.google.com

http://www.archive.org/stream/bookofhusb
andry00fitzuoft/bookofhusbandry00fitzuoft_dj
vu.txt

http://www.exclassics.com/ingold/ing18.htm

http://www.libraryireland.com/articles/Hall
DUM16-92/

http://books.google.com/books?id=ytJNRDL
0zDgC&pg=PA115&lpg=PA115&dq=origin+of
+the+idiom+not+a+dry+eye+in+the+house&s
ource=bl&ots=WKE5wNuH2_&sig=eQEmogf
XglrhZJ6NsCWSseom_Rc&hl=en&ei=U7hKTu
7-
E8rb0QH7stjqBw&sa=X&oi=book_result&ct=r
esult&resnum=4&sqi=2&ved=0CC8Q6AEwA
w#v=onepage&q&f=false

http://quod.lib.umich.edu/e/eebo/A59339.00
01.001?view=toc

http://webcache.googleusercontent.com/searc
h?q=cache:fOgGQsrsYJkJ:coxscorner.tripod.co
m/southpaws.html+history+of+left+handedne
ss+being+inferior&cd=2&hl=en&ct=clnk&gl=u
s&source=www.google.com

http://www.lib.muohio.edu/multifacet/recor
d/mu3ugb2544539

http://books.google.com/books?id=xCADAA
AAYAAJ&pg=PA1506&lpg=PA1506&dq=1904
+called+Life+in+Sing+Sing&source=bl&ots=G
4NzWxu8cm&sig=GFFpaV66gogEd2CX05Yle6
f-
Ywk&hl=en&ei=8f5PTqDTNOzD0AHw7MDf
Bg&sa=X&oi=book_result&ct=result&resnum
=3&ved=0CCwQ6AEwAg#v=onepage&q=190
4%20called%20Life%20in%20Sing%20Sing&f=f
alse

http://www.archive.org/stream/lifeandreala
dve00murrgoog#page/n6/mode/2up

http://books.google.com/books?id=pCADvln
bHFQC&pg=PA67&lpg=PA67&dq=Narrenbes
chw%C3%B6rung+(Appeal+to+Fools)+by+Th
omas+Murner,+Germany,+1512&source=bl&ot
s=SrYdghdCEb&sig=Z0YBYhZcHVh9JhKHOlc
bt_YPvaw&hl=en&ei=Mu9UTvXhJ4Ld0QG6nI
3JAg&sa=X&oi=book_result&ct=result&resnu
m=5&ved=0CDsQ6AEwBA#v=onepage&q=N
arrenbeschw%C3%B6rung%20(Appeal%20to%
20Fools)%20by%20Thomas%20Murner%2C%2
0Germany%2C%201512&f=false

http://www.yaelf.com/aueFAQ/mifsos.shtml

http://www.bookbrowse.com/wordplay/arc
hive/detail/index.cfm?wordplay_number=14

http://www.johnflorio-is-shakespeare.com/florio1.html

http://www.ebooksread.com/authors-eng/milton-oswin-percival/political-ballads-illustrating-the-administration-of-sir-robert-walpole-hci/page-22-political-ballads-illustrating-the-administration-of-sir-robert-walpole-hci.shtml

http://www.archive.org/stream/cihm_10654/cihm_10654_djvu.txt

http://books.google.com/books?id=9re1vfFh04sC&pg=PA57&lpg=PA57&dq=%22beyond+the+shadow+of+a+doubt%22%2B%22beyond+a+reasonable+doubt%22&source=bl&ots=JGWxlB9oUk&sig=tPcWQBRujZPOM9uPVbsUPTta1so&hl=en&ei=xALqSYHdDoH-swOJiuXkAQ&sa=X&oi=book_result&ct=result&resnum=8#v=onepage&q=%22beyond%20the%20shadow%20of%20a%20doubt%22%2B%22beyond%20a%20reasonable%20doubt%22&f=false

http://www.hmhco.com/

http://www.clansinclaircanada.ca/articles/beyond.htm

http://www.shakespeare-oxford.com/?p=10

http://www.clansinclaircanada.ca/articles/be
yond.htm#intro

http://www.newschool.edu/nssr/het/texts/c
arlyle/carlodnq.htm

http://www.wordorigins.org/index.php/foru
ms/viewthread/1404/

http://www.deepdyve.com/lp/edinburgh-
university-press/shackerley-marmion-redux-a-
second-look-at-the-soddered-citizen-
jW1XC2iZ69

http://originsofsayings.blogspot.com/2006/0
8/people-who-live-in-glass-houses-
should.html

http://books.google.com/books?id=9re1vfFh0
4sC&pg=PA517&lpg=PA517&dq=His+father+
pulled+some+wires+and+got+him+out+of+jai
l&source=bl&ots=JHTCowcf_k&sig=lFevqB3F
MtbsTnb45FyIWvz6k-
o&hl=en&ei=g0RmToyrNcHZgQfVtvCcCg&sa
=X&oi=book_result&ct=result&resnum=1&ve
d=0CBkQ6AEwAA#v=onepage&q=His%20fat
her%20pulled%20some%20wires%20and%20g
ot%20him%20out%20of%20jail&f=false

http://everything2.com/index.pl?node_id=10
14076

http://en.wiktionary.org/wiki/don't_cry_ove
r_spilt_milk

http://answers.yahoo.com/question/index?qi
d=2007070512

http://wiki.answers.com/Q/Don't_cry_over_
spilled_milk_origins#ixzz1XebZKvJL

15940115R00221

Printed in Poland
by Amazon Fulfillment
Poland Sp. z o.o., Wrocław